God 

Do you feel stuck? Have you felt like giving up on your dreams lately? I highly recommend Jeff Shortridge's book *God Honors Movement.* I've known Jeff for many years, and I've watched his life echo the profound and practical truths within these pages. There's nothing like learning from someone who's been down but discerned how to move forward. Jeff will teach you how to get up, get out and get free!

JENTEZEN FRANKLIN

Senior Pastor, Free Chapel
New York Times Best Selling Author

Many books can communicate an idea, but author, teacher and consultant Jeff Shortridge adds a treasure chest of gems along the way! He has the ability to bring both clarity with illustration and impact with interest. "God Honors Movement" is the core to what makes our faith viable. Read it, but also, read between the lines. You'll find a wellspring of wisdom and defining truths that line the pathway to a refreshing look at God's amazing grace!

DR. WAYNE CORDEIRO

Senior Pastor, New Hope Church
President, New Hope College

A wise thinker once stated, "All that is important is that one moment in movement". In this riveting and thought-provoking writing, Jeff Shortridge has captured the significance and the importance of that moment. This book is a flawless work and is most representative of God's mobility character with timing and purpose. If you are serious about making a difference with every moment and movement of your life and ministry, this is a must read. God does honor movement!

BISHOP SIR WALTER MACK

Senior Pastor, Union Baptist Church
Author, *Creative Ministry Moves*

I love endorsing a book when I know the author has modeled the book's message. That is true with this book and this author. Jeff Shortridge has written (and lived) a must-read message for anyone needing that final push to make your next move. The entertaining yet powerful testimonies of God moving for people, coupled with Jeff's unique ability to explain why God moved for them is both simplistic and profound. He brings clarity to the Biblical principles that will have you seeing the impossible become possible in your life, church, business, or ministry.

MARK COLE

CEO, The John Maxwell Company

Pastors and church leaders have found themselves forced to navigate through the uncharted waters of an ever-accelerating cultural shift, intensified by a global pandemic. The natural response in times like this is to allow our hearts and vision to become frozen and paralyzed by fear. In this book, God Honors Movement, Jeff Shortridge gives practical, biblical and very helpful insights that will greatly help leaders move their churches forward into the new, unprecedented opportunities awaiting us. I highly recommend it!

LEE CUMMINGS

Senior Pastor, Radiant Church
Author, *Be Radiant*

When you read through the most profound stories of the Bible, you will discover a common thread: Movement. As the leader of multiple organizations that serve churches and their congregations, I have seen this principle at work, both corporately and individually. As you read this book, I pray that you will be inspired to move toward what God has asked you to do. I am confident you will see, just like in the stories Jeff shares in this book, that God will honor your steps of faith.

JOSEPH SANGL

CEO, INJOY Stewardship Solutions
Author, *I Was Broke. Now I'm Not.*

GOD HONORS MOVEMENT

How Movement Leads to Miracles

JEFF SHORTRIDGE

All Scripture is King James Version unless otherwise noted.

Printed in the United States of America by Morris Publishing®
3212 East Highway 30, Kearney, NE 68847
www.morrispublishing.com

Published by NIN Publishing in Anderson, South Carolina

Cover design by Megan Hibbard

Library of Congress Control Number: 2021902242

Shortridge, Jeffrey

ISBN: 978-0-578-85247-8

First Edition

ACKNOWLEDGEMENTS

My greatest debt of appreciation and love is to God who has been so faithful to teach me one of the greatest lessons in life, that He truly does honor movement. On innumerable occasions He has personally escorted me into impossible situations, simply to let me see how amazing He can be when He comes through with a miracle. He must chuckle when he sees my surprise and wonder, each and every time.

My heart is filled with thanks to my wonderful bride for agreeing to spend her life with me and for being my biggest cheerleader while writing this book. Thank you for your input and willingness to proofread each chapter. Thank you for proving with me that God truly does honor our movements.

I am eternally grateful for my mother who raised me, not just with her words, but led me in the ways of God with her actions. It was watching her faith in God, coupled with her movement, that set me on the path to write this book. She taught me that when you move, God will honor your movement.

I am grateful for the pastors I have served who have inspired me to put pen to paper through their courageous movement. I am humbled that you allowed me to walk alongside you while you faced impossible odds with no apparent solutions. Watching you move and seeing God reward you with the miraculous has been nothing short of amazing.

God Honors Movement

Introduction

Have you ever stood in your driveway, looking at a broken-down car and wondered, "How in the world can I pay to get this thing fixed when I don't have two pennies to rub together?" Have you ever received a word of prophecy and, deep down inside thought, "Not sure that could ever happen?" Have you ever been faced with a business opportunity and thought, "I'm in over my head?" Have you ever felt compelled to take a step of faith, but when looking at circumstances, it seemed like a foolish risk?

I have.

I have felt my stomach churn in worry. I have felt my chest constrict with anxiety. I have felt my mind rebel, believing the necessary seems flat-out impossible.

But I have also experienced something else.

I have seen what happens when, in spite of appearances, I and others move forward in obedience.

It's strange but based on my experience (and understanding of the Bible) it seems like the smartest, strongest and most well-resourced aren't always the ones who accomplish the incredible. In fact, it seems like the most basic requirement for God's blessing is one simple thing: A willingness to go forward. A willingness to move, even if everything inside you is screaming to sit still until everything makes sense. God doesn't always honor expertise. But I do know this: God honors movement.

I want to be honest with you at the outset: I'm not really sure I'm the best guy to put pen to paper and share this message. I'm not a scholar. I'm not a prophet. The truth is, I'm just like a lot of you. I'm trying to take care of my wife and kids. I'm doing my best to pay the bills and grow as a Christian. There are those out there that have more letters behind their name and credits to their author biography.

But there is this one thing: I have lived the truth that I'm inviting you to experience. The message I'm about to share with you isn't something I read in a book. It's not something I learned in a classroom. It is a message that I have seen play out many different times, in my own life and in the life of many Godly leaders.

In some ways, I have the best job in the world. Almost daily, I have the honor of walking alongside some of the greatest men and women in the church today. Men and women that are leading churches into the next level of God's purpose. They are standing on platforms week after week inspiring people all over the world. These are people that God has personally entrusted to deliver a life-changing message to millions. For me, this is as equally humbling as it is rewarding.

For more than a decade now, I have been working as a coach and consultant. I have met with more than one hundred pastors and helped them figure out how to share God's vision for their church. I have listened as they shared their hopes, holding them out like a brand new puppy, wanting everyone to fall in love with this amazing bundle of possibilities. I have seen men and women make a move when it would have been easier to sit still.

I've also had the chance to live this truth. It started when I was just a child, raised by a mom who, in spite of having lost her husband in his early thirties, found faith enough to believe in movement. It continued when I was growing up, watching as the improbable was overcome by the inevitable of God's supernatural power. It was proven to me when, despite all appearances, a godly woman prophesied, "You are called to be a leader in business." Just a few months later, I found myself serving as the CEO of a multi-million-dollar resort. Time after time. Challenge after challenge. Hurdle after hurdle. I have seen something amazing play out. God honors movement.

Now, let me be clear. I'm not talking about easy believism. This isn't some "name it and claim it" formula for self-advancement. What I'm talking about is *movement in obedience*. When we obey God and take that next step, he will never let us sink.

Remember Peter? I imagine him squatting in that fishing boat with the other disciples. I can see that boat tossed up and down like a roller coaster. I can feel the water stinging his face, whipped by a stormy wind. He and his buddies are holding on for dear life as they see Jesus walking toward them, treading the waves like a guy on his morning stroll. At first, they think, it's a ghost.

"Jesus, is it you?" Peter cried out.

"Yep," said Jesus.

"Jesus, if it's you, tell me to get out of the boat and come to you."

"Come on out, Peter, the water's just right," Jesus chuckled.

Peter moved.

Everyone likes to focus on him sinking. But what I find so amazing is that this guy got out and felt what it was like to walk on the water. Jesus, who was God in human flesh, honored Peter's willingness to move.

In the next few chapters, I want us to take a look at this amazing, supernatural reality. I am hoping that as we do, you'll feel yourself getting fed up with a faith that sits still. I hope you'll feel a passion grip your heart. A passion that is willing to move. A passion willing to risk. A passion for God so strong that you really do believe nothing can stop you from fulfilling his plan for your life.

Along the way, we are going to be asking and answering three basic questions:

1. Why does movement matter?
2. What is the connection between faith and meaningful movement?
3. What does movement require?

My prayer is that you will read this book as an invitation from God, not just an interesting idea. God didn't save you simply to get you to heaven when you die. He saved you so that you could have a dynamic relationship with him, true friendship. That friendship is forged in the fires of movement. A life of meaning will be characterized by movement, for that kind of life brings God glory!

1

Why Does Movement Matter?

Before we spend time considering what God wants from us, it's important to begin by thinking about him. You see, everything we do will flow out of our view of God. If we have a small view of God, we'll be hesitant, fearful, worried. If we catch a glimpse of who God is, then we come to realize something: God has no limits.

For just one moment, imagine needing nothing. That's not as easy as it seems. I don't just mean try to imagine not needing a refrigerator full of groceries. Imagine not needing food, oxygen, or sunlight to survive. Imagine not needing a job or money. Imagine not needing medicine or medical help. Just think about what it takes for you to take that next breath.

Right now, I'm sitting on a chair, resting on a floor, built on the earth, spinning 88,000 feet per minute and flying through space at about 67,000 miles per hour. The precise tilt of our planet makes life possible. The exact distance between the earth and sun is fine-tuned for our existence. There are a nearly numberless set of variables that determine whether I stay alive from one second to the next.

In other words, we are *dependent*.

God isn't.

God doesn't need anything in all of creation to be God. He is the only self-contained Person. He's as happy as it's possible to be. He's as perfect as it's possible to be. He is perfectly content. He can make things happen simply by willing them to be. That's totally amazing.

That brings us to an even more important insight. You see, as we begin to consider why movement matters, the first thing I have to tell you is that all movement must flow out of a sense of awe and wonder. We should be amazed that God wants us to do anything at all!

Think about it: God could get it done without us, couldn't he? He could snap his fingers and whatever he wanted would spring into reality. That's what it means to be all powerful! God could get anything he desires without us. Right?

On one hand, this is true. On the other, it misses the point entirely.

You see, God doesn't just want a particular thing to happen. God cares about the *way* it happens. God doesn't just want us to achieve a task, he cares about *who we are* and the *way we go about* completing that task. This is the exciting part: God cares very deeply that we experience the fullness of his presence as we move.

As incredible as it sounds, the most amazing thing that God wants from us is our love and faith. More than the works we can accomplish. More than the ways we can innovate. More than anything else, God wants to be in a relationship with us, and He wants us to choose that relationship with him above anything else.

God doesn't just want to get things done. He wants people who love him to get things done. He wants us to freely love him more and more. The way he helps us do this is by meeting us as we move.

The reason God wants us to move is because it draws us closer to him. It leads us to lean on him. It helps us to know him in ways we otherwise couldn't know him if we just sat still and watched life pass us by. Movement that God honors flows out of our relationship with him and feeds into a deepening awareness of who he really is.

I see this working in two ways.

First, movement draws us closer to God by teaching us to trust him enough to take a risk.

When I was fresh out of Bible College, I found myself living in Athens, GA. One night I was about to climb into bed when I felt a sudden urgency to go to the Athens Regional Hospital. I felt this was strange and attempted to shake it off. It wouldn't go away. Finally I surrendered to the compelling inner voice, got dressed and headed to the hospital.

I found myself driving fast, working my portable electric razor up and down my face erasing the days five-o-clock shadow. I was praying with great intensity asking God what this was about. I had no idea what I was doing or why.

I arrived at the hospital and hurried through the sliding entrance doors. Walking up to the elevators and standing in front of the keypad I suddenly felt like I was at a dead-end street. I had no direction beyond this point. I said, Lord, what do I do?" I heard nothing, no voice, no prompting, absolute silence. I pressed the "up" button and walked onto the elevator. With no other plan I said, "Eeny meeny, miney, moe," and pressed the number of a random floor.

Exiting the elevator, I was once again awkwardly aware that I had no idea where I was going or why. I felt somewhat dumb and was thankful there was no-one in sight to wonder why I was standing there thinking of what to do next. I half-expected to feel some strong presence of God to manifest and give me a strong sense of direction. It didn't happen.

I was in a waiting area, so I walked to the door directly in front of me and pressed the button on the speaker. A distracted female voice crackled through asking, "May I help you?" "Clergy," I responded. The door buzzed open, and I stared down a long hallway. It was eerily silent, and many lights were turned down. I could slightly make out a small huddle of people standing outside of a room halfway down the hall.

I approached them slowly and could quickly see most were emotional. Several were crying, holding and consoling one another. I stopped alongside of a couple of the ladies and glanced quickly in the dim room. There was someone on the bed hooked up to several softly beeping machines. The room was full of people gathered around the bed.

I turned to the ladies beside me and introduced myself as clergy. I then asked if there was anything I could do to help. They immediately opened up and explained that all the relatives had been called in as this was the final hours of the elderly lady laying on the bed. I asked if they would like for me to pray for her. They immediately walked into the room and asked everyone to step aside. I moved to the bedside, looked down at the lady and then up at the family.

They were all staring at me. I assume they were wondering who in the world the stranger was. To this day I don't know what words came out of my mouth. I just started speaking and trusted God to give me the right words. I then turned to the lady and prayed over her as best I knew how. Saying amen, I stepped back out of the room and watched as, not five minutes later, she slipped into eternity.

Walking back to my car I understood why I had felt such urgency to get dressed and head to the hospital. I even understood why I had driven fast to get there. To this day I don't know what my actions did for that family. In all honesty, I think the beneficiary that evening was me. God had just taught me about being sensitive to His Spirit, obeying and moving when He said move. In doing so, he drew me into a deeper relationship with him. This relationship is founded in experience, not just an idea.

Second, movement draws us closer to God by granting power of anointing

God gives many people gifts, but not everyone experiences the power of anointing. Let me explain, using the story of two very different kings. One was named Saul, the other, David. Saul was Israel's first king, but he was rejected by God. David came second, but he was God's friend. One had gifts. The other had gifts *and* anointing.

Saul was a tall and attractive man. He was a people magnet, and a natural leader. He could even prophesy with the prophets.

Gifted people often struggle to stay humble. In a sense, they don't have to be humble to do what they do. It comes naturally without effort.

Gifted people come in two varieties. Some are born with natural gifts: singing, administration, music, dancing, speaking, finance. Then there are those who have been granted supernatural gifts: wisdom, knowledge, faith healing miracles, prophecy, discernment of spirits, tongues, interpretation of tongues (see 1 Corinthians 12).

This is the important thing to realize: The gifts and the calling of God are without repentance. The Holy Spirit will never be sitting around in your house in January and decide to take back the gifts he gave you in December, but he can decide that he doesn't want to commune with you anymore. The Holy Spirit is a gentleman, he won't harass you if you are not talking to him. Salvation is by grace alone. The gift of fellowship, however, is tied to obedience and ongoing pursuit of the Lord.

If you've been part of the church for very long at all, you have probably heard about or known a gifted person who flamed out. Maybe you were surprised or disillusioned. Maybe you were shocked and thought, "How could someone who preaches with such eloquence and passion have such a failure?" Simply put, it's because giftedness does not guarantee anointing.

Anointing implies relationship. Anointing flows out of really knowing and fellowshipping with the Lord.

There's an interesting parallel in the stories of Adam and Abraham:

- In Genesis 4:1 Adam "knew" Eve his wife and she conceived and bore a child they named Cain.
- In Genesis 16:4 Abraham "went in" unto Haggar and she also bore a son whom they named Ishmael.

In both these scenarios you have the same action which brought about the same result, a child. Only one of these situations had an actual relationship of intimacy. One is an expression of a deeper relationship of the heart that develops over much time spent with one another. The other is simply an action without the relationship.

It is possible to operate in the church, and even in your marriage, going through the same motions and getting similar results, yet never having a deep relationship.

There are people who win the lost, volunteer at church, bring their families to the house of God and even operate in ministry yet do all these things without an intimate relationship with the Lord.

There are those that have what looks like a beautiful marriage. They have a picture-perfect spouse, beautiful children, a nice house and all the trappings of a successful family. Then one day they announce they are getting a divorce. They had the same action and the same apparent results of those couples who have great relationships, yet eventually they tire out and quit.

There are those that operate in the gifts of the Spirit yet they themselves do not even "know" God in a relational and intimate way. There is nothing more sobering than this truth: Someone can have God's power without having His presence. We owe it to ourselves to ensure that we do not skip the presence and simply go after His power. In the words of Jesus, *"For what shall it profit a man, if he shall gain the whole world, and lose his own soul?"* **Mark 8:36**

Saul had it all. Saul had gifts, but he didn't have an anointing. He missed it because he drifted out of fellowship.

David, on the other hand, had gifts *and* anointing. David evidenced many different gifts. Some of them were obvious. He was a songwriter, capable of writing music that lasts even till today (having composed many Psalms). He was a leader and warrior, capable of drawing others to him and mobilizing them for action. David had amazing courage and administrative brilliance.

These things, however, were not the secret to David's success. At the very heart of who he was, David was a man who loved the Lord. After his failure with Bathsheba, when David lifted up a prayer of repentance, he knew he had wronged people. He knew he had broken God's law. But even more fundamentally, David knew he had damaged his fellowship with the Father.

> *Hide thy face from my sins, and blot out all mine iniquities.*
>
> *Create in me a clean heart, O God; and renew a right spirit within me.*
>
> *Cast me not away from thy presence; and take not thy Holy Spirit from me.*
>
> *Restore unto me the joy of thy salvation; and uphold me with thy free spirit.* **Psalm 51:9-12**

The source of David's joy was not the great things he could do. He didn't find purpose in performance. David longed for the *presence* of the Lord more than anything else. Why? Because the presence was the place where the anointing flowed! All his gifts, used without the anointing, would only accomplish temporary results, but movement with anointing would impact eternity!

David knew this, and we need to understand it as well. Movement for movement's sake is not the point. God wants movement to flow out of our relationship with him. That kind of movement, anointed with his divine power, will not only make things happen, but it will also make something happen in us. It will teach us what it means to be a child of God.

Movement for movement's sake is not the point. God wants movement to flow out of our relationship with Him.

In the following chapters, we will explore the dynamics of movement. As we do, let's remember the *purpose* of it all: To know God, our Father, in relationship. This is why movement matters. This is what he wants more than anything. And, if you don't mind me saying, it's what I want *for you*.

2

Movement Springs From Faith

So then faith cometh by hearing, and hearing by the word of God. **Romans 10:17**

But without faith it is impossible to please him: for he that cometh to God must believe that he is, and that he is a rewarder of them that diligently seek him. **Hebrews 11:6**

"Therefore everyone who hears these words of mine and puts them into practice is like a wise man who built his house on the rock." **Matthew 7:24**

Have you ever been on YouTube and come across one of those insane people who are into base-jumping? These risk-takers find big things, jump off them and trust a parachute or wingsuit to carry them safely to the ground. If you haven't seen it, you need to put this book down and check it out right now!

Question: How do they do this?

This question can be answered from a number of different angles. From one perspective, we could explain the physics of lift and drag. From another, we could talk about the physical training and preparation it takes. Or we could talk about the psychology of these crazy people (and trust me, they're crazy).

But all those considerations don't really get to the heart of the matter. Someone could have all those pieces in place and still, when the moment comes, refuse to leap. How do they do it? Well, at a very deep level, they have faith. They stand on a cliff's edge, or a skyscraper, or the narrow landing skid of a helicopter, look out and believe, "This is going to work."

Somehow, they bring themselves to a point of trusting in their training. They believe in the equipment strapped to their body. They trust that their calculations of height, angle, wind, and distances are accurate. They *believe*. If they didn't, then they wouldn't throw themselves into the adventure.

Have you known any Christians who make things happen? I don't mean they just have a forceful personality or crazy resources to throw around. I mean, they follow through. They take risks that seem a bit reckless, and those risks seem to pay off. Have you ever wondered, "How do they do that?"

On the other hand, have you known a believer who seems to resemble nothing more than a bump on a log? No movement. No momentum. At times, you're tempted to hold a hand mirror under their nose to see if they're still breathing. Have you ever wondered, "Why are they like that?"

Faith is the X-factor in both of these situations. One person has it. The other does not. Sure, they might have the

If you want to

EXPERIENCE

the blessings of movement,
you must
realize something:

It

STARTS

with faith.

basic faith to trust in Christ for salvation, but for some reason, that faith has never matured and strengthened.

One person's faith tips the scale and leads to movement. The other's does not.

If you want to experience the blessings of movement, you must realize something: It starts with faith. It starts by *truly believing* what God has said. With faith, anything is possible. Without faith, nothing's going to happen.

Where Faith Comes From

This is important: Without faith, there is no movement. That's another way of saying what the author of Hebrews 11:6 wrote, *"Without faith, it is impossible to please (God)."* Faith is the ingredient that makes it happen. Like gasoline in the car. Like nutrients in our body. Like love in a mother's heart. Faith is essential. So how do we get it?

Some people think of faith like an emotion. It comes, and it goes. Have you ever tried to make yourself feel something you weren't feeling. Not easy, is it? Is faith like that? Is faith like the first puppy love we experienced that wore off and never really came back?

No, it's not.

Paul told us in Romans that faith comes by *hearing the Word of God*. Now, if you've been in any relationship, especially if you're married, you know there is a world of difference between hearing and *listening*. Sometimes, you can be sitting with someone, pouring out your heart only to realize that they've been casually checking out their cell phone the whole time. They've been hearing the words, but they haven't really been listening.

It's like that with God. He's speaking. In fact, he's speaking all the time! How often are we listening? It can be like that with our devotions—zooming through that psalm and forgetting what you read just a few minutes later. Or with the preacher's message—your body is in the room, but your mind is at the beach.

Faith comes from hearing that is really listening. Let's break this down a little. There are two essential ingredients for growing faith.

The first essential ingredient is: The Word of God. There is no substitute for the Word. God used words to make the world. God spoke and formed a nation out of Abraham. God, the Word made flesh, came into this world and won our salvation. The Word brings God's life into our lives.

The Word is like a seed. Have you ever planted a garden? Some find sheer joy in doing this, and it's mind-blowing to contemplate. Midway through the time of harvest, you walk through rows of tomatoes and see fat, red, juicy goodness growing on vines. Everywhere you turn, there's life just waiting to be picked and turned into food.

But it starts with the seed. Think about that seed. It's small, just a tiny, dry-looking thing. When you shake it into your hand from a seed packet and look at it, you are looking at a miracle of creation. In that seed, smaller than a pebble, lies a design plan that causes the plant to grow, burst with new fruit, and produce hundreds more seeds. It just needs to be put into the ground. Try doing that with an I-Phone and see what comes up. As amazing as our technological innovations are, none of them can hold a candle to that simple seed.

That's what God's Word does. It is the seed that carries his plan. It alone holds the Divine DNA for new life. We can't have fruit that remains without the seed of God's Word in our hearts.

It is important that we grasp the full range of what we mean when we talk about God's Word. At a foundational level, we mean the Bible. The Bible is God's Holy Word in written form. As Christians, we believe that God inspired every word of Scripture. Sure, he used people to do it. He used all kinds of people—farmers, doctors, fishermen, scholars and kings. God oversaw that entire process in such a way that, when it was all said and done, everything they wrote was exactly what he wanted. There is no other source of revelation with such perfection and authority.

But this isn't the only way God speaks. The Lord also speaks to us through the Holy Spirit *using* that Word in our life. Have you ever been reading the Bible, and it seems like a passage just jumps off the page, wraps itself around your heart and gives it a good squeeze? That's because the living Holy Spirit is drawing from God's written word to give you a *right here, right now* word in your life.

God also speaks to us in other ways. Sometimes, he will speak directly into our heart and give us a revelation. At others, someone with a prophetic gift will speak into our lives. God can even use dreams to speak. Of course, that word will never contradict His written Word, but we need to respect the words that God gives us. I learned that from my mom.

Mom's Well Runs Dry

When I was a young teenager, my mother was widowed and parented her five children on her own. We lived in a small three-bedroom, one-bathroom ranch house on the edge of a corn field. Because we lived in the country, we did not have access to city water being piped into our home. Instead, we had a well that had been drilled down deep into the earth where it tapped into a fresh-water stream.

One day, the water coming out of our faucets began turning dirty. The kitchen sink, the bathtub, the toilet, it all began to run dark ugly water the color of Maryland soil.

My mom shared the scenario with our Pastor knowing that before his ministry calling, he had been a plumber. He listened to the symptoms and did a quick mental diagnostic then paused before sharing the bad news. He said, "Sister Shortridge, your well has run dry. The only way to get good water flowing through these pipes again is to call a well drilling company and have them drill down deeper until they find another freshwater spring."

My mother was horrified. She asked, "Is that going to be expensive?" The Pastor responded that it indeed had the potential to cost thousands of dollars.

When my father unexpectedly passed, he did not have life insurance. This left our family with no funds to survive on except Social Security. We knew what it was like to not know how the bills were going to be paid or where we would get Christmas gifts from. We didn't have health insurance. We drove cars that were half broken down and would catch fire at the drop of a hat. We didn't go out to restaurants and always wondered what it was like to go on a real vacation. Clothing itself was a challenge to come by and without the help of relatives we would not have had those nice new outfits every year.

Drilling a new well was not even a possibility. My mother's saving account consisted of a $100 bill hidden in a wallet, in a spare purse in the back of her closet.

A day or so after receiving this news about our well, we went to church as was our custom to do at least three times a week. Our congregation had just finished moving into a new church building and had run out of money before there was carpet on the floor and paint on the walls.

There was a visiting minister speaking in the service that evening, and he took note of our unfinished place of worship. At the end of his sermon he said, "It's not right that we have carpeted and well-furnished homes, and the house of the Lord sits undone." He continued, "The money is in the house, and we are going to take up an offering." He then asked everyone to pray about what they should give.

My mother, the saint that she was, bowed her head and prayed. She asked the Lord what her part was to be. He immediately responded that she was to give the $100 bill in her closet.

What Will You Do With the Word?

How would you have responded if you were in my mom's situation? It all depends on whether you value the seed of God's Word. Do you really believe that it can do what he says it can do? More importantly, do you really believe he *is* who he says he is?

When the Word of God comes, it has the power to produce movement, but that can only happen if we do more than *hear* it. We have to *listen*. Just as the seed does no good stuck in an envelope, the Word must go down into the soil of our hearts. Only then will it produce faith that allows the divine Word of God to bear fruit in our lives!

That brings us to the second *essential* ingredient for growing in faith: We can't get anywhere without the seed, the first ingredient, but the seed can't do anything until it is planted. We must *receive* the Word. We must *trust* the Word. And then we must *act* on that Word. This is how faith grows.

We must receive the Word.
We must trust the Word.
And then we must act on that Word.

My mom taught me this through her actions.

After hearing the Lord call her to surrender her last $100 and being acutely aware that she had a new well to dig, she found faith. This made all the difference that night in church.

She began to weep as fear knocked on her heart's door. She prayed, "God, this is all the money we have. If the kids need shoes or a dentist appointment or the car needs repaired, this is all we have left!" Then she remembered the greatest need that was creating her unneeded stress and followed up with, "God, we need a new well! We don't even have water in our home!"

The Lord's response was almost instantaneous. He said, "How many feet do you think you can drill down with $100?"

She wept as her heart yielded to the Holy Spirit. She took a tithe envelope out of the pew in front of her and wrote a pledge that she would give $100.

When we arrived home after church that evening, I remember running into the house and into the kitchen. Out of habit, I grabbed a glass out of the cupboard and turned on the water spout for a glass of water. Immediately, strange sounds began to come from the faucet as air and dirt pushed its way through. Suddenly, fresh spring water began streaming through that kitchen faucet.

We never had to hire a drilling company, never had to spend a dime on a plumber. My mother listened to God and acted in obedience. She took care of God's house, and He took care of her house.

Of course, I'm not claiming that giving $100 will always translate into a material benefit, but I am saying this: Movement takes faith. Faith comes when we *listen* to the word God speaks into our lives. The more you do it, the more you will want to do it.

God didn't save you so you could sit around like a bump on a log. God has mountains for you to climb. He might even want you to jump off one of them. As crazy as it may sound, any one of us can do that when we embrace God's Word with a heart of faith. Didn't Jesus say something about actually *moving* mountains with faith? Faith the size of a mustard seed, right?

3

God's Word Always Comes to Pass

Seek ye the Lord while he may be found, call ye upon him while he is near: Let the wicked forsake his way, and the unrighteous man his thoughts: and let him return unto the Lord, and he will have mercy upon him; and to our God, for he will abundantly pardon. For my thoughts are not your thoughts, neither are your ways my ways, saith the Lord. For as the heavens are higher than the earth, so are my ways higher than your ways, and my thoughts than your thoughts. For as the rain cometh down, and the snow from heaven, and returneth not thither, but watereth the earth, and maketh it bring forth and bud, that it may give seed to the sower, and bread to the eater: ***So shall my word be that goeth forth out of my mouth: it shall not return unto me void, but it shall accomplish that which I please, and it shall prosper in the thing whereto I sent it.*** **Isaiah 55:6-11** (emphasis added)

As I type these words, America and the entire world is in the midst of a crisis. It's 2020 and the Coronavirus has swept across the globe. Schools have been shut down, businesses closed and thousands of jobs lost. Even more troubling, millions have been infected and many thousands have died from this deadly virus. All of this has been made much, much worse by a worry many of us have. I'm sure that, as you remember this time, you felt it too. What is this worry?

Simply put, we don't know if the experts really know what they're talking about! Am I right? One moment, we're told that masks are not effective. The next, we're told everyone needs to wear one. We're told that this disease is deadly to a very limited number of people. Then we watched as our entire society was placed on lockdown. People were confused, and it was no wonder. Everyone was asking, "Do we really have a solution here?"

Our world is a big complex place. If we stopped to think about that, it might be difficult to make decisions. After all, we rarely have all the facts. Inevitably, we have to move forward, knowing that some unaccounted-for factor could throw our plans into turmoil.

If only we could have a perspective that takes all things into account. If only we could rise above the noise and see the big picture. If we could, then we'd have an incredible advantage.

Think about it. Imagine you could see everything that is happening right now. For a moment, imagine you had a super-computer that would analyze every bit of data and produce a reliable prediction of what comes next. What would you do with that kind of power? Play the lottery? Invest in the stock market? Maybe plan a vacation to the one place on planet earth with perfect weather for ten consecutive days?

I want you to know something. You have something much better than a computer at your disposal. You have a source of perspective, wisdom and knowledge that sees *everything*. In fact, this source does much more than observe. This source sovereignly controls the events of history and takes every detail into account, right down to the number of hairs on your head.

I'm speaking, of course, about Google. Just kidding! Even Google isn't that powerful. There is only one source of such knowledge, and it is not a company or computer. It is our Creator.

Here is good news: Our Creator is also our King. Through salvation in Christ, we have been brought into *his* reality. We have been aligned with *His* purposes, and, this is the really exciting part, we have access to *His* perspective.

Let that sink in for a moment.

Climatologists have access to a limited data set. From that, they make predictions. Historians dig through records of the past. Archeologists sift through the sands of time. All of them are looking for information to form a theory. We know the God who has numbered every star in the sky and every grain of sand in the Sahara. He even knows the number of hairs on your head.

That same God has chosen to reveal himself to us. He has chosen to speak to us in such a way that we can see things as he sees them. Of course, from our limited perspective, there are countless factors we'll never take into account. But we have a secret advantage: We know the one with unlimited perspective and unfathomable power.

What does all this mean? Very simply, it means we can totally trust the Word of God. In the last chapter, I talked about having trust in the Word. In this chapter, I want to *fuel* that trust by helping you see that God's Word *always* comes to pass. By fueling that fire, you'll be able to push through moments of doubt and confusion.

I can't say enough about this: Your conviction that God's Word *always* comes to pass will absolutely determine your willingness to move and *keep on* moving when things get hard. It's not enough to acknowledge the idea. It's not enough to nod your head and say, "Amen." We need to firmly establish this truth in our thinking so that it constantly influences the atmosphere of our mindset.

That's one of the reasons the Lord has given us examples in Scripture. We read stories of faith that astound and inspire us. One such story is the life of Joseph. Joseph showed us what it looks like to believe God's Word, even when the going gets tough.

God had given Joseph a dream that he was going to be ruler over his brothers. He saw them bowing at his feet. He later had a second dream, this one indicating that his parents, along with his brothers, would one day bow before him. Joseph knew that both of these dreams came from the Lord. They were God's Word to him, but Joseph's faith in that Word was put to the test over several long, heartbreaking years.

It began with the ridicule and eventual betrayal of his own brothers. You can just imagine what *they* thought of Joseph's dreams. To say it led to some bad blood is an

Your

CONVICTION

that God's Word

ALWAYS

comes to pass
will absolutely
determine your

WILLINGNESS

to move

and keep on moving
when things get hard.

understatement. It led them to sell their brother into slavery.

Though his brothers laughed at him, Joseph believed.

After serving with distinction as a slave for a prominent Egyptian, Joseph was falsely accused of sexual assault. He was thrown into prison. Can you imagine? God's Word seemed light years away from fulfillment.

Even when he was living in a prison, Joseph didn't throw in the towel. He continued to minster, interpreting dreams and helping the prison keeper.

Here's the amazing thing: At what might have been the lowest point in his life, Joseph had no idea just how close he was to seeing God's Word come to pass! He was six months away from being the prime minister of Egypt and everything still looked the same. He was three months away from being Prime Minister of Egypt and nothing had changed. In fact, when he was one week away from having a royal escort into the palace, there was nothing around him to confirm that he was making any progress towards seeing his dream fulfilled.

In these moments, we all have a choice. Will we trust God's Word, or will we give into our doubts and feelings? Will we define our future by our current circumstances? Will we, like so many "experts" define our expected outcome according to our own perspective or will we elevate? Will we rise above the horizon of our own viewpoint and look at things from God's vantage point?

Again, the most amazing truth in the universe is this: God gives us that option! In Christ, we have been granted a place to stand. From that place, we can see much further than we would on our own footing. We have a perspective that even the Hubble Telescope can't compete with. We gaze not just across space but through time. Why? Because we know something: If God said it will happen, then it *will* happen!

If God said it will happen, then it will happen!

That place of perspective is the realm of revelation. It is the realm opened up to us through Scripture. It is the realm opened up to us through the Holy Spirit, who breathes into us through Scripture and causes that word to come alive *for us*. It is the realm opened up when we fellowship with the Lord and listen to his voice. From that place of perspective, we can *know* the things God has in store for us:

> *For I know the plans I have for you," declares the Lord, "plans to prosper you and not to harm you, plans to give you hope and a future. Then you will call on me and come and pray to me, and I will listen to you. You will seek me and find me when you seek me with all your heart.* **Jeremiah 29:11-13 (NIV)**

God gave these words to Israel to sustain them at their lowest point, when they were slaves in Babylon. Just as Joseph was given a word to sustain him through the trials he would face, God gave Israel a prophetic revelation that would assure them of his good plans while they were in exile.

That is what the Lord wants to do for you.

What he wants *from* you is a willingness to trust in His Word, even when it seems like nothing is happening. Trust him enough to know that he is working, even if you can't see it. Just because things still look the same around you, it doesn't mean there is no progress. Joseph stayed faithful while God was lining things up for him.

You see, as Joseph looked around at his circumstances, he was going nowhere fast, but he *trusted* the word that had been given through that dream long ago. Though he could not see *how* God was doing it, he wisely trusted that God was going to fulfill his promise.

You remember what happened next, right? Pharaoh, the greatest emperor in the world at the time, had a dream that shook him to his core. It was a dream rich with symbols and significance, but he could not interpret it. God knew just the man for the job. In fact, he had conveniently brought him to Egypt for just this moment!

Even when we don't understand God's process, we should never doubt his Word. It was God who gave Pharaoh the dream that perplexed him to such a degree that he couldn't rest until he could find someone to provide an interpretation. While some people would have thought, "God's given up on Joseph," Joseph knew, "God's just lining things up." Who would have been right? Who could have predicted God's word would come to pass through the Pharaoh of Egypt?

It was important that Joseph did not give up on God or his promises during this process.

One of the questions you might have is: Why does God so often take us through such a process on his way to fulfilling his Word? That takes us back to chapter one. Remember, God is not just about outcomes. He is about *relationship*. He's taking us through trials to teach us something so important: We can trust in his love and obey his word. As crazy as it sounds, we don't always do a good job of believing that.

When God is working with people, things might feel like they take a little too long to come to fruition. Sometimes things do take longer if the Lord has to develop those involved so that they are ready for the time when it arrives.

God was preparing Joseph, not just for an important position, but for the second highest position in the land. Joseph not only needed the position, but he also needed to be the right kind of man when he reached it. God also had to bring Pharaoh to a place that he would have such a level of respect for a prisoner, that he would readily place him in a place of leadership second only to him. And lastly, I believe God enjoyed displaying His glory to this influential emperor as He worked out his Word in Joseph's life.

God is a gentleman. He doesn't always just demand people do something but instead develops circumstances around them that will guide and grow them in the right direction.

Our experience of his guidance will entirely depend on whether we trust the Lord to fulfill his Word. If we do, then we will go through every trial with a sense of hope and confidence. I'm not saying it won't hurt, but I will say it's the difference between getting sore feet from taking a majestic hike and getting a sore toe by stubbing it in the dark. One is a chosen journey with a destination. The other is a random event that leaves you hopping in pain. One requires effort and perseverance. The other just seems like the Universe is out to get you.

When we trust and keep on trusting, we can be sure God's Word will come to pass. Along the way, we'll get to know him better, and that is what life is all about.

4

God Never Ignores Prayer

And in the morning, rising up a great while before day, he went out, and departed into a solitary place, and there prayed. And Simon and they that were with him followed after him. And when they had found him, they said unto him, All men seek for thee. And he said unto them, Let us go into the next towns, that I may preach there also: for therefore came I forth. And he preached in their synagogues throughout all Galilee and cast out devils. **Mark 1:35-39**

And he spake a parable unto them to this end, that men ought always to pray, and not to faint; Saying, There was in a city a judge, which feared not God, neither regarded man: And there was a widow in that city; and she came unto him, saying, Avenge me of mine adversary. And he would not for a while: but afterward he said within himself, Though I fear not God, nor regard man; Yet because this widow troubleth me, I will avenge her, lest by her continual coming she weary me. And the Lord said, Hear what the unjust judge saith. And shall not God avenge his own elect, which cry day and night unto him, though he bear long with them? **Luke 18:1-7**

Typically, my job requires a lot of time flying from city to city. I've become accustomed to packing a suitcase, traveling to the airport and hopping on a plane. As a regular traveler, I also know that weather can majorly impact my plans!

Perhaps the most devastating kind of natural phenomenon is a hurricane. These incredible storms can build up to heights of 50,000 feet and span hundreds of miles. Their fierce winds blow between 74 and 157 miles per hour. They can transport and deposit immense amounts of water. For instance, Hurricane Florence dumped 9 *trillion* gallons of rain as it swept across North Carolina in 2018, an amount equivalent to half the volume of the Chesapeake Bay! The impact of the massive storms can hardly be overstated. Each year, they steal lives and destroy billions of dollars of property.

Imagine being able to harness the power of such a phenomenon and direct it for creation rather than destruction? We haven't figured out how to do such a thing, though science has learned much about how these storms arise. As warm, moist ocean air over the equator evaporates, it rises, is cooled and when conditions are right, forms an ever expanding, rising column of air. As it begins to rotate, there is a multiplier effect, causing even more warm air to rise, be cooled, form clouds and create conditions for a massive storm.

In other words, it comes down to the *environment*. Storms don't arise by accident. The right conditions at the right time make the hurricane possible.

In this chapter, I want to tell you something: You *do* have the power to harness a hurricane. Actually, something much more powerful than a hurricane. God has invited you to be part of creating an *atmosphere of possibility*. He is inviting you to lend your purpose and intention to establishing an environment. Just like the conditions that give rise to a hurricane, this atmosphere is powerful beyond belief. Jesus showed us that those who move out in this atmosphere of possibility can heal the sick, raise the dead, walk on water, deliver people from demons, see prison walls fall and watch gravestones get rolled away in the light of resurrection!

How do we create this atmosphere? There is only one way. It does not come through your efforts. It does not come through simply wanting it. It does not come through anything you can plan and execute. This atmosphere is created in one way: Prayer.

Prayer is the only thing that establishes this atmosphere of possibility. Why is that? Because prayer is the ultimate expression of faith. Prayer is the voice of God's children saying, "We trust you, Father!" Prayer is the cry of a heart that wants God's *super* on our *natural*!

Remember what we've been learning so far: God is not just trying to get us to do things. He is seeking to draw us into a relationship of trust in him and his word. He's using the unfolding days of your life to bring you closer to his heart. *Faith* is the act of trusting in him. *Prayer* is the fundamental expression of a heart of faith.

When we pray, we are bringing together the key elements of God's supernatural movement in this world *through us.* Just as a tornado touches down and causes the mighty power of a vast storm system to be expressed at ground level, prayer causes us to become a focal point of God's divine power in this world.

How does prayer do all of this? I want to show you three ways that prayer allows God's power to move in and through us.

First, prayer creates an atmosphere of purification. The psalmist writes:

> *Who shall ascend into the hill of the Lord? or who shall stand in his holy place?*
> *He that hath clean hands, and a pure heart; who hath not lifted up his soul unto vanity, nor sworn deceitfully.*
> *He shall receive the blessing from the Lord, and righteousness from the God of his salvation.*
> **Psalm 24:3-5**

We can't move where God wants us to go when we are hanging on to sin in our lives. God wants us to run after his purposes, but if we're caught up in negative patterns of behavior and belief, it's like wearing shackles. The best we can do is shuffle along.

The good news of this Psalm is that *Jesus* is the one with clean hands and a pure heart. He is the only one who deserves God's blessing. But through faith, we inherit *everything* that Jesus does! So we are allowed to ascend the hill of prayer into the presence of God. We are *cleaned* and *purified*. We are *set free* so that we can follow him.

Prayer aligns us with these fundamental realities of faith. Prayer opens the door for the Father, once again, to remind us that we are part of his family. It allows us to enter into his presence. That place of his presence leads us to the second thing prayer does.

Second, prayer creates an *atmosphere of discovery.* Here's another powerful psalm:

> *Blessed is the man that walketh not in the counsel of the ungodly, nor standeth in the way of sinners, nor sitteth in the seat of the scornful.*
> *But his delight is in the law of the Lord; and* ***in his law doth he meditate day and night.***
> *And* ***he shall be like a tree planted by the rivers of water, that bringeth forth his fruit in his season****; his leaf also shall not wither; and* ***whatsoever he doeth shall prosper****.* **Psalm 1:1-3**

This psalm shows us what happens when we enter into God's presence. It's interesting. The English version talks about the "law" of God being the subject of our meditation, but it goes even deeper than that. In the original Hebrew, it's not just the written Ten Commandments. It is the *ways* of God, the *purposes* of God, that are in view.

The place of prayer is a place of discovery, because here, in his presence, we discover what God has intended for our lives. He unfolds his plans for us. Sometimes, those plans are something we never could have imagined! I remember once when someone gave me a word. It was a word shared with me out of a place of prayer--the atmosphere of discovery.

There was a precious white-haired, elderly lady that attended a church where I was on staff. She was the kind of lady that if she said the Lord told her it was going to rain, it didn't matter if the sun was shining, I was going to carry an umbrella. Her name was Beverly Bartlett.

She had a unique way of giving you the word God had spoken to her spirit; she would write it in poems. She eventually packaged a large portion of her poems in a book titled, "The Lord's Garden," and it can be purchased on Amazon.

One day I was standing in the foyer of the church and Miss Beverly approached me. She said God had given her a word for me and then pulled a piece of paper out of her Bible. She unfolded it and began to read the most beautiful poem. I immediately realized she was prophesying over my life. Following is a portion of it:

> *You won't have to walk this path alone.*
> *I have chosen a mate for you.*
> *Someone to share your every desire*
> *To make things bright and new.*
> *Together you'll bring me much glory,*
> *As you preach and teach my word.*
> *Signs, miracles and wonders will follow*
> *Wherever your voice is heard.*

Many years later, I was preaching in Knoxville, TN, and I was subsequently introduced to a beautiful young lady who, a couple of months later, I messaged on Facebook. I asked if she would mind if I called her. She responded the same day by sending her cell phone number.

It was New Year's Day, and I called her that evening. That proved to be more than the first day of a new year; it became the first day of the rest of my life. We have spoken every day since then.

I'm grateful God gave Miss Beverly that word of encouragement for me. To be truthful, I was very discouraged at the time. I was in my thirties and had never been married. I had spent many years believing God for my Proverbs 31 woman to do ministry together and spend the rest of my life with.

How did Miss Beverly get that word? It happened in an *atmosphere*. That atmosphere is created through prayer, conversation with the Lord. Within that atmosphere, God's divine love reached out and provided a word for my life. That atmosphere of discovery is just what we need to *get moving* in our lives. When we experience the Father's love, as he shares his purposes with us, we are *moved and motivated*. This leads to the third thing prayer does.

Prayer creates an *atmosphere of activation*. As we practice the presence of God in prayer, we discover something: Faith must always be manifested in works. Our faith, boosted by the experience of God's presence, launches out into action. This is what I mean by an atmosphere of activation.

In reality, It didn't matter how much I wanted a wife, or how many people God sent to me to let me know He was working for me. If I had not executed action when the time was right, I would not have received my miracle wife. I had posted that poem in a frame on the wall in my office, but if I hadn't picked up my iPhone and reached out to her, I might still be single. You see, Faith without works is dead.

Without works, faith dies on the doorstep of hope, believing for a miracle but never getting up and obtaining it.

Without works, faith dies on the doorstep of hope, believing for a miracle but never getting up and obtaining it.

I believe there are words that have been spoken over people and over churches that have not yet manifest because God is waiting on His people to take action. When we enter into prayer, we create an atmosphere of activation. And when that happens, God will work in ways that we never could have imagined.

As I write this, it's a Saturday morning, and my wife and I just had a monumental moment in our home. I was sorting through a handful of mail that my son Tony brought in from the mailbox. In the stack was an envelope from a church we spoke at several weeks ago. My mind couldn't piece together why I was receiving a letter from them.

When I opened the mail, I simply couldn't speak. My bride was watching me and saw the look on my face. She asked several times what the letter said before I was finally able to read it to her. It was typed out with an old-fashioned typewriter. Enclosed with it was a check. We both stared at each other with huge smiles of astonishment. Our oversized smiles belied the absolute elation we felt inside. It wasn't the check itself, but rather the combination of the amount and timing of the check.

Not too long before that we had made a commitment before the Lord, and to each other, to fund a major financial goal that would have huge long-term impact on our family and ministry. We knew it would take a lot of extra effort and focus. An acquisition of this nature had to be broken up into multiple steps and wins throughout a specific timeline.

The night before we opened that envelope, we were doing the math and realized that we were a lot closer than we thought to reaching a major milestone on this journey. We went to bed excited at what God was doing through us. Little did we know that the very next morning we would not just be closer to this milestone, but we would be staring at a check which would completely put behind us the completion of this incredible increment!

It was not just a check we were looking at; it was a word straight from God that He was honoring our movement, that he was putting his super on our natural. That he was paying close attention to the details of what we were doing financially and was in the game with us.

Can I say that there is no feeling in the world like knowing God is literally in the game with you, working on your behalf?

In the letter, the Pastor stated specifically that the Lord ministered to him to send us this sizable check. Only God knew what we were doing! Only he knew the precise timing that would communicate to us the message he was trying to deliver. He was honoring our movement.

We had posted a piece of paper on our bathroom wall with a financial goal for each month. It was a tremendous vision and audacious to say the least, but my wife had been listening to the Lord. She strongly felt that this was what he was telling her. I was more than willing to give it a shot. We had no idea how we were going to make this happen, but we started.

My bride drew a grid of each month and wrote a prayer at the top. She said, "God, help us reach this amount every month to finance our vision." Then she wrote down the big audacious number.

A day or so later she came back and wrote the two words "more than" before that number.

Only a few days later, my wife was at work when the manager called her into the office. There she was informed that she would be receiving one of the largest raises in her department.

When we set out with our financial goal in mind, we had no idea God was going to begin matching our movements with miracles, but he did. Just like when the Israelites marched around Jericho. There was a wall, and there was a word. They did not immediately see results, but they kept moving. God honored their movement.

Where does all of this start? It *must* start in prayer. That is the place where God works in us, purifies us, fellowships with us and propels us into movement. Prayer *must* be the engine of your movement, or you'll never really experience what happens when God puts his super on your natural!

5

God Brings Promotion Through Obedience

But in a great house there are not only vessels of gold and silver, but also of wood and clay, some for honor and some for dishonor. Therefore if anyone cleanses himself from the latter, he will be a vessel for honor, sanctified and useful for the Master, prepared for every good work. **2 Timothy 2:20-21** (NKJV)

He spoke another parable, because He was near Jerusalem and because they thought the kingdom of God would appear immediately. Therefore He said: "A certain nobleman went into a far country to receive for himself a kingdom and to return. So he called ten of his servants, delivered to them ten minas, and said to them, 'Do business till I come.' But his citizens hated him, and sent a delegation after him, saying, 'We will not have this man to reign over us.'

"And so it was that when he returned, having received the kingdom, he then commanded these servants, to whom he had given the money, to be called to him, that he might know how much every man had gained by trading. Then came the first, saying, 'Master, your mina has earned ten minas.' And he said to

him, 'Well done, good servant; because you were faithful in a very little, have authority over ten cities.' **Luke 19:11-17** (NKJV)

The year was 1989. I was just 17 years old, and I remember it like yesterday. I was standing in the hall of our church just outside the pastor's office. There was a Pepsi vending machine against the wall displaying the 1980's Pepsi logo and branding. The pastor leaned against it, absent-mindedly jostling a set of keys. I was in a special season, aggressively seeking the heart of God as to what I was going to do with my life after my high school graduation.

As I poured out my heart to the pastor, I shared how I thought the greatest thing to have the opportunity to do would be traveling around the country and visiting churches everywhere. I simply wanted to see how they did things.

He talked with me about going to Bible College. He thought it would be a great idea for me since I felt a call to ministry. For some reason I was not a fan of the idea.

I had a passion to do *anything* that would further the kingdom. I was teaching Bible Studies, delivering the message when my pastor asked me to do it. I did it all: Leading worship, teaching Sunday School, picking people up and bringing them to church with me, helping build the new church building. Whatever I could do to further the Kingdom, I did it!

It wasn't just performance, however, that interested me. I wanted desperately to go to the next level with God, although I had no idea what that would look like. I came to a place where I felt that if I didn't find God's leading for my next season, I would curl up and die inside.

We finished construction of our new church building and scheduled a grand opening. It was a night of celebration and worship and people came from everywhere. The auditorium was packed. A world-renowned Gospel artist was invited to lead worship.

The special evening service was scheduled to begin at 7:00 sharp, but when the appointed time arrived, our building was packed with everyone *except* the Gospel artist who was scheduled to perform.

My pastor was thinking fast. He looked at me and said, "I need you to do something for me." I asked, "What's that?" He said, "I need you to go up there and lead the crowd in some worship until our music guest arrives."

May I just take a moment to say that it is an intimidating day when you are kid that no-one knows, and you're asked to walk on the stage where everyone there is expecting to see and hear a nationally renowned artist. I stared at my Pastor, processing the situation he was putting me into. I nervously nodded my head in agreement and began looking for the house band. We quickly assembled with the worship team and began a chorus of praise.

It was nearly 45 minutes later that the Gospel artist and his band showed up. They had experienced a major traffic delay. When the Dove Award winning artist walked into the building, there I was on the platform, singing the best I knew how. I have never been so happy to see someone in my life! I knew I was not the one this crowd had traveled there to see.

I closed out my song and announced to the congregation that the artist had arrived. The applause was thunderous as the band walked through the back doors. Everyone was cheering and whistling.

Buying time so the group could get set, I had the people fellowship with each other while the road crew wheeled their commercial sound equipment into the auditorium. Big, heavy black road cases were whisked down the aisle. Speakers were hoisted into the air. Keyboards appeared on stands, and drums flew onto center stage. A massive cable was rolled down the center aisle to connect the house sound mixing console to the stage mixing console. It was an incredible process.

I had never seen anything like this and neither had the crowd of people sitting in the sanctuary. They were getting a lot more show than they had anticipated. It was fascinating to watch these pros do their thing.

If you are familiar with bands setting up sound equipment at venues, you know a spectrum analysis is needed before they begin operating. Without it there is sure to be lots of feedback, rings and roars. And so, it began. White noise was flooded through the house as they set the EQ's to match the acoustics of the room.

The moment the noise was turned down the drummer slipped behind his kit. Then, the keyboardists each sat down behind their state-of-the-art keyboards. Each musician and singer slid into place.

When that first note rang out and the drums started, the place went crazy. The energy in the room was so electric that everyone was bursting with shouts of praise. It was one of the most memorable moments of my life.

At the end of the concert, the pastor hosted the artist and his group at a dinner on another part of the campus. Being part of the ministry, I was invited. It was there that the artist invited me to come to the Bible College where he was dean of music. He had watched me lead worship and work with the crowd to help prepare the atmosphere for him. He requested I submit an application for a scholarship.

I had never been fond of going to Bible College, but over the next several months the Lord dealt with my heart. Here I was, facing a decision to do exactly what my pastor had encouraged me to consider. I had been serving, pouring out my time and doing whatever I could. Now, I was being asked, "Jeff, are you willing to obey?" After being accepted for a partial scholarship, I enrolled in Bible College for the beginning of a whole new era in my life.

So now you may be wondering what that whole story had to do with God-honoring movement. If you remember, I was at a place emotionally and spiritually that I felt was a dead end. I wanted to go to the next level but had no idea what that looked like or how to get there.

In the middle of a small crisis, I was asked to make a move that I had no idea was coming. I accepted the challenge and moved instantly to help my pastor out of a jam. God honored that. It was from that decision of movement that a Dove Award-winning Grammy nominee saw me, and God used him to take me to the next level.

It was ironic that only a year later, I myself was recruited and traveling with that same artist.

I share this story to make one simple point: We never know exactly when or how obedience will lead to promotion. Only one thing is sure: When we faithfully obey the Lord over time, it will take us to a new level.

That's what Paul told his disciple, Timothy. Using the image of different vessels in a home, he encouraged Timothy with a basic principle: When we seek the righteousness of obedience, God purifies our hearts. He moves in us. Even when we can't see it, he can see us. When he sees a heart that is surrendered to obedience, the Lord sees a vessel that can be put to honorable use.

Jesus made the same point in his parable about the stewards. In that parable, the master gave a task, then disappeared for a season. The servants didn't have his visible presence to guide them, but they did have the last thing he had given them: His instructions. Those who obeyed were rewarded.

When I reflect back on my life, I can see how these principles have played out every single time. I can't predict where, when or how the promotion will come, but the law of promotion has proven true again and again. God isn't looking for the most talented people. He isn't interested in our personal brilliance. What he seeks is our obedience. When we move in obedience to his commands, God takes notice.

The most important movement we can possibly make is to obey what the Lord has shown us in spite of circumstances, our comfort levels, or what other people might say. If we obey in the face of these obstacles, the Lord will see it.

The most important movement we can possibly make is the move to obey what the Lord has shown us.

God is so very good that he can't help but pour out some of that goodness on our obedience. Always remember this truth: Obedience brings promotion.

6

God Honors Sacrifice

Give, and it will be given to you: good measure, pressed down, shaken together, and running over will be put into your bosom. For with the same measure that you use, it will be measured back to you. **Luke 6:38 (NKJV)**

I beseech you therefore, brethren, by the mercies of God, that you present your bodies a living sacrifice, holy, acceptable to God, which is your reasonable service. And do not be conformed to this world, but be transformed by the renewing of your mind, that you may prove what is that good and acceptable and perfect will of God. **Romans 12:1-2 (NKJV)**

Therefore we also, since we are surrounded by so great a cloud of witnesses, let us lay aside every weight, and the sin which so easily ensnares us, and let us run with endurance the race that is set before us, looking unto Jesus, the author and finisher of our faith, who for the joy that was set before Him endured the cross, despising the shame, and has sat down at the right hand of the throne of God. **Hebrews 12:1-2 (NKJV)**

Here's a spiritual principle you can take to the bank: Whenever people give to God, He blesses them. Scripture supports this in Luke 6:38, *Give and it shall be given unto you, pressed down, shaken together and running over.* Those words are an iron-clad guarantee from a King who never lies.

I have a thought that just might blow your mind. What if we decided that being blessed was not enough? What if we became hungry to see the miraculous? What if we desired to see the supernatural power of God working visibly, tangibly in our lives? I believe there is a way it can happen. It lies along the path of sacrificial obedience.

There is a kind of movement that leads to the miraculous. When you move past simply giving of your time, talents, and treasure; when you move for God because you took time to listen to His voice and sacrifice out of obedience, you move beyond being blessed. You transition into the miraculous.

Many times when God asks you to do something it will entail a sacrifice. It might be a spiritual or psychological sacrifice--our pride, selfishness, dignity, or dreams. It might be a physical sacrifice--our comfort, sleep, or even our sense of safety. In those moments, we must choose the way of sacrificial obedience if we want to enter the realm of the miraculous

When you step into the realm of moving in sacrificial obedience you step into the realm of the miraculous. We see this principle everywhere in the Bible.

1. Abraham – Because he was willing to sacrifice his only son, he became the father of millions.
2. Widow of Zarapeth – Because she was willing to give her last meal to the prophet, her entire

household was sustained through the rest of the economic downturn.

3. Naman - Because he was willing to sacrifice his pride by dipping in the river, he was healed of a terminal illness.

All through scripture you find that God honors sacrificial obedience even more than gifts. We know it is true that that... *if you give it shall be given unto you, pressed down shaken together...*

I am concerned we are coming into an era where people are afraid to make these kinds of sacrifices. Maybe we have become too soft, too comfortable. In fact, in the minds of some people, this kind of sacrificial obedience just doesn't make sense. That's why I want us to think about it together. Because, actually, it makes all the sense in the world.

Sacrifice of Obedience

First, it is critical to understand that we are never asked to sacrifice just for the sake of sacrificing. Some Christians get the idea that if they make themselves uncomfortable, they'll get God's attention, and therefore his blessing. This is no different than the prophets of Baal who cut themselves with knives in the hope their false god would act on their behalf (see 1 Kings 18). We worship Yahweh, not Baal. Our sacrifice is never made because we're trying to get God's attention or manipulate his will.

Sacrifice is required as a response of obedience to God's revealed will. Scripture draws a line of distinction

Scripture draws a line of

DISTINCTION

between those who

ACT,

and those who

ACT OUT OF OBEDIENCE

between those who act, and those who act out of obedience. God doesn't move miraculously just because you make yourself uncomfortable. He often requires you to push through discomfort on your way to the miraculous. God is looking for sacrifice in correspondence with obedience.

When you act, you can receive a blessing. We see an example of this when Noah acted in obedient sacrifice and his entire family was saved from annihilation. Had he built whatever he wanted he would have been blessed with the joy of looking back and seeing his handiwork. That in itself can be rewarding. Yet, because he constructed what God said to build, he was more than blessed. A supernatural intervention manifested before him.

There are four things I see that triggers God to put His super on your natural:

1. Take time to get away to a quiet place and listen to His still small voice. Here you will receive directions.
2. Obey the instructions God gives you
3. Generally, when God instructs you to do something, it will require a sacrifice.
4. Act on that sacrifice in faith.

These are the four things I have seen that produce miracles. In this specific order.

Too many people just move because they are inspired or motivated by a movement around them. They might feel peer pressure or be coerced by a compelling speech. No doubt when you act, you feel the blessing of making a difference, but that is not always the movement of obedience. It alone cannot bring God's supernatural into our natural.

Moving Through Fear

One reason people do not or will not move forward is that they feel they have too much to lose. In other words, they are paralyzed by fear. At some level, they have come to believe that whatever God asks them to give up is worth more than what he wants to give them!

This is rooted in a deeper problem—trust. Ask yourself a question, "What kind of Father do I believe God really is?" Is he a stingy father who withholds? Is he a demanding father who can never be pleased? Is he a selfish father who only asks but never gives?

Of course, Scripture and our own experience makes it clear that this isn't true of God at all! In fact, God proves himself again and again to be a God who wants more for us, not less. We can *always* trust that what God wants *for* us will always be exponentially greater than what he asks *from* us. Whenever we are asked to sacrifice, we should be rubbing our hands together with excitement. It means that God's got something great on the horizon! If only we had faith to believe it.

The Rich Young Ruler

The rich young ruler came to Jesus wanting to understand how he could be saved. He had kept all the rules. He was a good boy. I wonder if he was expecting Jesus to say something like, "You've already done it! In fact, all you need to do is join my band of disciples. I'll make you my right-hand man."

Instead, Jesus looked into that man's soul and knew he needed something. He needed to see the relative worth of all his possessions and performance in comparison to the prize of being accepted by God's amazing grace. The only way he would actually realize that was by giving up those possessions and setting aside his performance.

"What must I do?" the man asked.

"Sell all you have, give it to the poor and follow me," Jesus replied. In another word: Sacrifice. This was the *move* the man needed to make if he wanted to move beyond a "blessed" life and into the hall of fame of history, forever known as the one that walked beside the Son of God Himself.

We will never know what this ruler lost by not following Jesus, but here is a thought. This young ruler was the 13th person to whom Jesus said, "Follow Me." The first twelve all followed him and became disciples. They each radically impacted the entire human race from that moment on. All because they moved when Jesus said move.

Peter, Andrew, James and John left their boats. Matthew left behind his tax collector's booth. Simon the Zealot gave up his fight against the Roman Empire. In one way or another, each of the men who followed Jesus were willing to sacrifice in order to obey Jesus' call to follow him.

Now, this is a bit of speculation, but I think it's worth consideration. Judas became the one and only lost disciple. He cashed in his place for thirty pieces of silver. He sacrificed the Son of God for some cheap trinkets. We know how he ended up.

Consider the rich young ruler. I wonder, when Jesus offered this man the privilege to follow him, did he plan to have him take the place of Judas? Did Jesus have an incredible destiny for this certain young man that was forfeited simply because he wouldn't make the sacrifice of obedience? Would there have been a book in the Bible named after him? We will never know. All we know is that his part in the Gospel story stopped when he declined Jesus' offer.

There is no record of him changing the world or leaving a legacy. There are no gospels written by him. We don't even know his name. As far as we know, he brought no glory to God from that moment on. How tragic. All his wealth and even his good works are lost to history.

This young rich man made an initial move to connect with Jesus, but then he came to a place where he determined that he could not make the necessary sacrifice to continue on to where Jesus had called him.

Did he worry that he had too much to lose? The rich young ruler came to Jesus. What must I do? Jesus said sell all you have, give it to the poor and follow me (move forward). If only he had understood that the blessings of the Kingdom would far outweigh anything demanded by a sacrifice of obedience.

Where the Sacrifice Starts

I'm convinced that one of the key problems for many of us starts right between our ears. In other words, with our mindset. Living in this world, we need to realize we're constantly under the influence of messages that the Enemy uses to control our thinking.

We live in an age of mass media, where every second we are not sleeping, information is being beamed at us through television, computers, phones, billboards, social media, etc. Most of these messages have a common theme: Get what you want to be happy. Be a consumer. Take. Keep. Hoard. Store up. Protect. Enough stuff will bring you satisfaction.

This can lead to a mindset that makes sacrifice seem silly. Why would any normal person choose a little pain when they could experience some pleasure? Why would we give up something good for something hard? Why would we choose to be uncomfortable when our pantries are full, our next Netflix binge is waiting and our beds are so dog-gone comfortable?

But all of these feelings are, in fact, rooted in fantasy. We must fight against the stronghold of comfortable consumerism if we want to enter into the realm of God's supernatural favor. It is an illusion that more stuff will bring satisfaction. It is a myth that accumulation leads to greater happiness. The truth is that only God can provide the joy and peace we're looking for. Wherever *he* is, that's where we should want to be.

We must cultivate a mindset that says, "I'm not going to get fooled by the mirage of momentary ease!" When we put our focus back on who God is, we suddenly realize that it is silly *not* to sacrifice if the result is something better than we have right now. That is his promise to us.

If we have any doubts about that, just think about Jesus. What did the Father ask him to sacrifice? The throne he had occupied for eternity. A limitless existence for flesh and blood. The worship of angels for the wishy-washy loyalty of twelve sometimes clueless disciples. And, of course, his ultimate sacrifice. Jesus sacrificed his dignity, his skin, his blood, his life. No sacrifice God demands from us can compare with the sacrifice he made for us.

Jesus didn't do these things because he was a masochist. The Father didn't demand this because he was a sadist. God enacted this incredible event because He is a *realist*. He believed that the prize was worth the price. What was the prize?

It was us.

You. Me. The world.

Wow.

Jesus' sacrifice on the Cross was followed by the miraculous—an empty grave! His sacrifice of obedience was rewarded with an eternal Kingdom, filled with citizens who understand what it means to be loved. The sacrifices he asks from us on our way to inheriting that Kingdom is what will teach us what it means to love Him back.

So, remember, the sacrifice of obedience is always worth making. It is the most important move we can make. Embrace it. You will never regret making that decision.

7

Movement Requires Motion

"For My thoughts are not your thoughts,
Nor are your ways My ways," says the Lord.
"For as the heavens are higher than the earth,
So are My ways higher than your ways,
And My thoughts than your thoughts.
"For as the rain comes down, and the snow from heaven,
And do not return there,
But water the earth,
And make it bring forth and bud,
That it may give seed to the sower
And bread to the eater,
So shall My word be that goes forth from My mouth;
It shall not return to Me void,
But it shall accomplish what I please,
And it shall prosper in the thing for which I sent it."
Isaiah 55:9-11 (NKJV)

God honors movement. This is not a Field of Dreams ("Build it and they will come") approach, this is much different. I have seen people make radical moves and expect God to jump right in with them. I've seen people build big church buildings only to never see them fill up and eventually lose them. I've seen people spend countless hours, week after week, month after month, praying and believing God for a specific person to be their spouse, but when they made a move on that individual it quickly became very obvious that God was not anywhere around.

To see God respond to your actions you must be aligned with His directives. If you are, then you will see God move, and the *way* he moves will often surprise you.

The key to this is very simple and is found in John 2. This key will keep you from stepping out into something and finding nothing there. It will also keep you moving forward, even when the way forward seems strange.

> *"And the third day there was a marriage in Cana of Galilee; and the mother of Jesus was there and both Jesus was called, and his disciples, to the marriage. And when they wanted wine, the mother of Jesus saith unto him, They have no wine. Jesus saith unto her, Woman, what have I to do with thee? mine hour is not yet come. His mother saith unto the servants, Whatsoever he saith unto you, do it.*
>
> *And there were set there six waterpots of stone, after the manner of the purifying of the Jews, containing two or three firkins apiece. Jesus saith unto them, Fill the waterpots with water. And they filled them up to the brim. And he saith unto them, Draw out now, and bear unto the governor of the feast. And they bare it.*
>
> *When the ruler of the feast had tasted the water that was made wine, and knew not whence it was: (but the servants which drew the water knew;) the governor of the feast called the bridegroom, And saith unto him, Every*

man at the beginning doth set forth good wine; and when men have well drunk, then that which is worse: but thou hast kept the good wine until now. This beginning of miracles did Jesus in Cana of Galilee, and manifested forth his glory; and his disciples believed on him." **John 2:1-11**

Jesus and his disciples were attending a wedding in Cana. Jesus had not yet begun his ministry. He came to the wedding with no intention of being anything more than a spectator. It was after the ceremony and the reception was taking place that they ran out of wine.

Here is what intrigues me. We are not told that they *needed* wine, simply that they *wanted* it. I'm fascinated by the fact that the first miracle Jesus ever performed was for a want not a need. Remember, when we see the face of Jesus, we understand the heart of God!

When Mary addressed Jesus regarding this problem, he did not make a move. In fact, He was a little brash with her stating, "What do I have to do with thee?" His initial response seems to indicate he has no inclination to act.

So what moved Jesus? What propelled him from his life of relative obscurity into open ministry? What moved him to pull back the veil on his divine calling and demonstrate his supernatural, Kingdom power?

I think I know the answer: It was a handful of guys standing in front of Him with the attitude of "whatever you tell us to do, we will do it." We know this because the servants were lined up waiting for his orders under Mary's directive: "Whatsoever He saith unto you, do it." Jesus looked into their faces and saw faith, and God loves to reward faith. This simple approach pulled Jesus from an entire lifetime of never performing a miracle to years of Him manifesting His glory.

Back to my original question: What's the difference between movement that God honors and movement that leaves you hanging? There is a huge yet uncomplicated difference between stepping out and finding nothing and stepping out and finding something. When you have a word from God and you have the tenacity to obey it, He will honor your movement 100% of the time.

When you have a word from God and you have the tenacity to obey it, He will honor your movement 100% of the time.

I want to remind you that because you serve the only living God, you can't pray without him hearing you. You can't honor Him without him honoring you in return. You can't resist temptation and not be rewarded. When we move in response to God's instructions, he moves heaven and earth.

Rio Revolution

When I think about this kind of movement, I'm reminded of a pastor I've had the honor of working with over the last few years. I met Pastor Pacer Hepperly after receiving an invitation to visit Rio Revolution Church in Maryville, TN. It was the start of a long friendship.

In the course of one of our conversations he began to share how he had launched the church just five years previously. The first three years were incredible. Rio Revolution grew by leaps and bounds. Miracles were happening everywhere. People were being saved, delivered from terrible addictions, and restored in their marriages.

But for two years, they had experienced a different story. For some unknown reason, they hit a growth wall. They couldn't figure out what the problem was. They had not eased up on evangelism. The services were just as impactful as they had always been. The music was incredible, and the sermons were relevant and anointed. Yet with all their efforts, growth had come to a grinding halt.

Can you imagine the discouragement? At some level, whether it's pastoring a church or just trying to move forward in life, we all know what it feels like to hit a wall. We look for solutions. We try to identify problems. Pastor Pacer and the other Elders tried everything, but most of all, they prayed very earnestly.

One evening Pacer sat in the living room of his house and talked with his wife. He expressed how it wasn't working out the way he thought it would. His voice was laced with discouragement. The enemy was assaulting him with doubt.

Pacer's wife was concerned. This kind of talk was rare to say the least. He was naturally a very upbeat, faith-filled and optimistic person. Two years, though, is a long time to not see noticeable growth in your church. Again, whether or not you're a pastor, you probably can imagine what it feels like to be pouring yourself into something without seeing fruit.

Rio Revolution was still meeting in a public-school auditorium but had purchased several acres of ground to build a church home. Looking back, Pacer could date the slowdown in growth to immediately *after* they had purchased this land. That seemed odd. What were they supposed to do?

A lot of people, encountering such setbacks, might backpedal. They might try to reverse what they perceive to be an earlier mistake or undo a step of faith. Pastor Pacer understood that the just don't live by sight, but by faith.

> *Now faith is the substance of things hoped for, the evidence of things not seen.* **Hebrews 11:1**

He trusted that when God gave him the vision to build, God also knew the congregation was going to hit a growth wall. God knows the end from the beginning. Pacer and the Elders determined they would move forward with raising the needed money to build a church home. They launched a capital campaign.

As soon as they launched the internal planning for their campaign, growth came to beat down their door. Visitors started showing up out of nowhere. Salvations and baptisms skyrocketed. Within 90 days, attendance increased 45% by adding 150 to the current 330 attendees.

Within five weeks of launching the campaign publicly to the congregation, they had 88 salvations. The exact day they announced the total dollars raised and committed to the new building, they saw eight people give their life to Christ.

There were many miracles happening. Beyond the salvations that were taking place, generosity was exploding. $157,254 came in in cash and $1,631,634 was received in faith pledges. The leadership base began expanding with quality leadership.

Over the following twelve months, the congregation tripled in size! Their story did not end there, however.

I spoke with Pastor Pacer as I am writing this book, and Rio Revolution has experienced so much growth that they recently began working on renderings for a new 2,000-seat auditorium. As they explored what it would look like to implement these plans, roadblocks appeared everywhere. Things kept hindering them. Something didn't seem to feel right.

At that moment, they could have stopped moving. But they didn't. Why? Because they knew God was leading them to do something, so they kept seeking the next right move. They chose to keep moving down the path the Lord had given them, but they did so with wisdom and care.

Pastor Pacer called their church administrator and said, "I want to slow this process down." They pumped the brakes and called the architect to put the signing of his contract on hold.

While they were discerning, God was directing! Just over a month later, Pacer's phone rang. It was a fellow pastor from a local church, calling to invite him for lunch. Over their meal, the pastor opened up, saying "I'm 62 years old and planted this church 16 years ago. I'm tired. I want to transition from pastoring to working in outreach. I talked to my trustees and discussed with them giving our building to outreach."

His church was sitting on four acres with a large, beautiful sanctuary. And the situation was even better: The facility and property were completely debt-free.

You see, this pastor had been watching Rio Revolution Church reach out and impact their community. He began asking around, learning more about Rio Revolution. Everyone he spoke to delivered the same positive report.

He looked at Pacer across the table and said, "God spoke to me and told me I need to give our property and building to your congregation."

Of course, that didn't mean the transition was without any roadblocks. This pastor's board, initially excited about the opportunity to fuel Kingdom outreach, got cold feet. The enemy came in, and the trustees changed their minds. They waffled.

The pastor never changed his mind though. He knew he had heard from God. It was *his* turn to keep moving forward in faith, even in the face of obstacles. He asked if Pacer would be willing to meet with the trustees. Pacer met with the trustees three times, but it was enough. Following their final meeting, the trustees agreed and closed the deal.

Just a short time before, Rio Revolution had been facing a roadblock that seemed insurmountable. Now they had another church building and property, debt free! This was an answer to prayer as the outreach they were doing could not be contained with their original campus. The story doesn't end there!

Within two months another businessman in town called. He said he had a piece of property he wanted Pacer to come look at. It was an old assisted living facility, with sixteen beds. This business owner had heard about Rio Revolution too. In particular, he had learned they were making an impact in the world of recovery ministry. He invited them to come take a look.

Frankly, Pacer was not interested at first. He was reluctant to even make the trip out to the property. Responding in faith, he grabbed a couple of staff members and drove to the property.

As they pulled in the driveway the Holy Spirit began talking. One of the staff members immediately started crying. Explaining herself, she shared that since she was a child, she'd had a vision for a home just like the one they were looking at. She had dreamed of a place that would minister to mothers who had lost their children into the foster care system, helping them take the steps necessary to be reunited with their kids.

Again, the Lord showed up. Though the property was listed at $1.1 million, God had something else in mind. By his favor, Rio Revolution was able to buy it with cash at a substantial discount! The ministry was expanding.

God's favor extended far beyond simply purchasing the property. Knowing it would need to pass the zoning commission, Pacer called the mayor. Whereas before, the local government had made the dream of expanding their current facilities difficult, this time, there was total synergy.

The mayor thought it would be an incredible idea to transform this facility, resonating with the dream to help minister to mothers of foster children. He brought Pacer to the zoning board and *insisted* that they help fulfill the vision.

Let's go back to the beginning of this testimony. What did we see? A church at a plateau, up against a growth wall. What changed things? A willingness to keep moving forward in obedient faith! Sometimes, faith means surrendering our version of God's plan.

You see, when Pacer and the church leaders listened to God's voice and "pumped the brakes," when they stopped moving with the vision they were already invested in, that's when God started moving in a much bigger and more diverse way.

When they said no to what they saw, God said yes to what he saw.

Now, Rio Revolution Church has an additional church campus, a gift from God. After a few renovations, they launched their first service. I bet you're not surprised to hear that it was 90% full on week one.

They also have a newly renovated mother's home called Reunite, also a gift from God. As of my last phone call they were 30 days away from moving in their first mom.

They have all of this, debt free.

God's ways are much bigger than our own!

What I have observed take place in Maryville TN is an incredible example of how God will introduce His supernatural assistance when you are walking in God-directed movement. Sometimes, when things aren't working out and we are hitting roadblocks everywhere, it might be a good idea to "pump the brakes" and check back in with God to see if He has something better.

This doesn't mean we stop moving. It just means we move in the right direction, towards the face of God! Many times, when it feels you are facing the greatest opposition, you are actually in a season where God is doing the most (behind the scenes) work to open a bigger door for you. When the waters of Jordan were backed up by the hand of God, they didn't recede to accommodate the Israelites crossing over. The spiritual leaders moved first by stepping into the rapid waters, at the peak of flood season. Only after they made that move did God respond with movement of His own; he stopped the water up and let them pass through.

Let this be an encouragement to your faith. Smith Wigglesworth, the British evangelist, once said, "Faith is just the open door through which the Lord comes." If you keep the faith, you will see God come through for you, I promise.

8

Movement Requires Stillness

Trust in the Lord with all your heart,
And lean not on your own understanding;
In all your ways acknowledge Him,
And He shall direct your paths.
Proverbs 4:5-6 (NKJV)

Have you ever seen someone wearing one of those shirts with an elegant crown and the words, "Be Calm And Carry On"? There are modified versions of this shirt, but the common message is, "Chill." That's important for people who want to move.

Sometimes the best movement is being still. Does that sound like a dichotomy?

Scripture tells a different tale. David said in Psalm 23:2 *"He maketh me to lie down…"* Psalm 46:10 says, *"Be still and know that I am God."* It's important to realize that this man who valued stillness was, by character and temperament, a man of action. When his mind was set on something, he preferred not to sit around and wait. He liked to get things done and make things happen.

A good example is 1 Chronicles 28-29. Here David caught the vision of building God a House of worship. He went "all in" and started gathering funds and resources to construct this palatial edifice.

God had other plans for David. While the Lord gave him the go-ahead to make necessary preparations for building the temple, he did not allow David to move forward with actually building it. During his life, David had been a man of war. The Lord wanted someone to build his Temple whose hands were not covered in blood. So God chose David's son, Solomon, to build the temple. Though David developed the plans and stockpiled the resources that were used to build it, we now know of the completed project as *Solomon's* Temple.

It is interesting that God had to stop David from building the tabernacle. In this case he was not to build, but he was to *prepare*. There are times when God puts up his hand and says, "Stop." But even in those times, God is often moving us forward, even if it feels like things are still.

I don't know that I have met a Pastor who received a God-given vision, yet was told not to do it in his lifetime. I have seen, however, God move and modify that leader's *understanding* of the vision. At times I've witnessed visions manifest into something different from, yet similar to the original plan. This happens in the context of *moving forward* in pursuit of the vision. What do these times of stillness mean?

Stillness Permits Preparation

There are times when God will not permit you to take the actions you want to take. This is hard for those of us who like to get things accomplished fast. In these cases, it is interesting to see that instead of God giving you the go-ahead for your intended project, He diverts you to preparing for the project.

If you have ever built a house, business, or church building, you know there is a lot of preparation that must first take place. There is knowledge to be gathered regarding architects, builders, zoning and building codes etc. If you have ever pastored a church or run a business, you know there is a tremendous amount of learning that must take place for you to be effective. Some of that learning may be book knowledge but many times it also includes the school of hard knocks. Long before there is realization of the dream, there is the refining fire of preparation.

As I have watched Pastors undertake massive church growth projects, I realize that most times God allows us to go through a process rather than just dump the finished product in our lap. That's because preparation allows something bigger to happen. We not only are able to accomplish a task, but we are also brought to a new place.

Preparation Leads to Places

My cousin Alvin is a petroleum engineer. He is also an avid hobbyist. He excels in almost anything he puts his hand to—electronics, welding, carpentry, modding. A few years ago, he decided he would build a Personal Computer that would be worthy of being published in a magazine.

It took him over 18 months to accomplish what he set out to do. In a forum on www.thebestcasescinario.com he explained that the length of time was mostly due to, "I didn't know much to begin with." He immediately entered into a huge season of preparation. Some of his preparation involved gathering materials while some of it involved connecting with others who could mentor him. He found an industrial designer and sought knowledge while also doing in-depth research in a multitude of other areas. In my conversation with him he listed off a plethora of skills he picked up during this preparation—etching copper, laser-cutting metal, working with Styrene, wiring circuits and glow wire, just to name a few.

When the PC was finally complete, he had turned a 1951 Zenith H664 Cobra-Matic phonograph into a powerful gaming computer. He sent pictures and specs to a national magazine publication, and it landed itself squarely on the front cover of CPU Magazine. A check also landed promptly in his mailbox.

Along the way, Alvin also learned something else: the outcome of his work was much more than a computer. The very process of preparation led to all kinds of fruit. What Alvin shared with me was profound. He stated, "Preparation leads to places." I think that's true for anyone who faithfully walks through preparation.

There are so many things that can happen along the journey of preparation. Each one of them opens the door to something bigger than simply finishing a task. All of them allow you to make a supernatural impact. Some of those include:

- You can mentor others who will follow in your footsteps, allowing the Kingdom to be multiplied through you.

- If done well, you can inspire others to not just do what you did but blow it away, pointing people to God's *abundant excellence.*
- You have invested in your personal vault of knowledge and skills, opening the door to still greater influence.
- If you don't give up, you actually have a desired finished product, providing a testimony of perseverance that will inspire others.

Notice I listed obtaining the completed product last. I did that on purpose because, in the end, the most valuable things you will get out of taking on a project is the investment you will make in yourself and the investment you will directly and indirectly make in others.

Alvin continued, "Sometimes the question is not, 'Did I hit my goal?' but rather, 'Am I a better person because I took the journey?'" He shared that the goal was to build a modified case for a computer. The journey, though, proved to be more rewarding than the completed project. While he has not pulled that innovative gaming computer off the shelf in a couple of years, what he learned along the way he has used in a hundred other scenarios since.

After walking alongside so many Pastors that are undertaking massive projects, it occurs to me that sometimes when God asks you to push pause on a project, He is not actually asking you to stop. In fact, he's asking you to *get ready!* Just like first-time parents who use the nine months of a pregnancy to prepare for welcoming a new life into their world, God is preparing you to welcome his new purposes into your world!

Sometimes He is divinely guiding you into a season of preparation that will build the absolute necessary foundation for you to then execute your primary vision. That preparation can come in different forms. Let's look at three.

Sometimes when God asks you to push pause on a project, He is not actually asking you to stop. In fact, he's asking you to get ready!

Physical Preparation

I live on the East coast. I have traveled to Hawaii to minister several times. Each time I have gone, there have been five services over two days—two on Saturday evening and three on Sunday morning. That's a lot. Now, add another interesting wrinkle that Hawaii's time zone is six hours behind my home state. This means I am usually giving my altar call for the second Saturday evening service at around 3:00 AM back home.

I've learned an important lesson. This trip requires physical preparation. My custom is to fly into Honolulu on Thursday and make myself stay up a few hours late that night. On Friday, I find myself waking up very early as I am still functioning on Eastern Time. Sometime during the afternoon, I take a one-hour nap and then push myself through that last adjustment, finally going to bed on

Hawaiian Standard Time. By the time I reach Saturday, a quick power nap in the afternoon enables me to make it through two sermons full of life and energy capped off with a heart-felt appeal for the lost.

As much as I want to simply fly to Honolulu, get off the plane and preach, I must prepare. I must first make myself lie down at times that I would prefer to stay up and then stay up at times that I would prefer to lie down. Take a second and ask yourself this question: How is this similar to our walk with God?

Financial Preparation

There are many occasions where financial preparation is the most important factor to consider. I have worked with many churches that have God-given, great visions. After sitting down with pastors and leaders of nearly 150 churches, I have discovered that the vision is much greater than the resources in almost every case. To tell you the truth, I love it when this happens. In my opinion, any pastor that is worth his weight has a vision that is bigger than his realized provision. I know I am sitting in front of this pastor because he knows that God can supply the need. He also realizes something else: Getting the right counsel is critical in executing the vision.

When a church is looking to build a new facility that will cost five to six times their annual budget, there must be a season of financial preparation. Unfortunately, some pastors wait until their current facility is bursting at the seams before preparing financially for the next build, purchase or renovation. When they fail to prepare financially, they usually forfeit a much more valuable commodity: Time. Acquiring the funds for a down payment on their loan can often require twelve to twenty-four months.

The cost can be more than time. Sometimes, the delay means stalled growth and ministry impact! This can cost them precious growth and winning of souls. Rev. Matthew Watley, senior pastor of Kingdom Fellowship AME Church, phrased it best when he said, "You can reach a season where your growth begins to hurt your growth."

At some point, wise leaders must learn the lesson of financial preparation. In a perfect world they would have been monitoring their church growth year to year and evaluating the pace of their annual growth trend. With that in mind, they would be able to predict a capacity wall and know when to begin financial preparation.

I recall working with Radiant Church in Jackson Michigan. Pastor Mike Popenhagen determined that with the current rate of year-over-year growth, his congregation would reach capacity by the fall of the coming year. He was looking at maximum capacity in the children's area, adult sanctuary, parking, social space as well as ingress and egress areas for service transitions.

Thankfully he had been preparing for this, placing funds in savings and acquiring architectural renderings to show his congregation. To ensure the renovation and expansion would happen successfully, we launched a capital campaign to assemble the final needed funds.

When a church fails to predict an inevitable wall of capacity looming on the horizon, it can place in jeopardy their God given momentum. This can be avoided by simply taking time to look back at what God has been doing and anticipate that he will not only continue the good work but will do greater than what we could ask or think.

People Preparation

Sometimes, God just needs to prepare *people* before they're ready for the next thing! Several times I have seen God "seemingly" slow down a build process in the middle of constructing a magnificent new facility. During this season, the staff and leadership base was expanded and strengthened. When they finally moved into the new facility the growth of the church skyrocketed and that new structure of leaders was able to manage and retain the growth. Had they attracted all those new people prematurely, many new conversions might not have been retained in the Kingdom.

Remember, God is always in action. He is always on the move. There is a reason he says, "Be still and know that I am God." You must do something in the process of that stillness. Sometimes it's as simple as letting your faith rise to the level of realizing that He is able to accomplish what he wants to do through you. Without the proper faith He cannot and will not act. Without faith it is impossible to please him.

When We Ignore Preparation

Preparation is so important to God. The greater the value of the project, the greater the preparation. Jesus talked about this, sharing a short analogy:

> *"For which of you, intending to build a tower, does not sit down first and count the cost, whether he has enough to finish it – lest, after he has laid the foundation, and is not able to finish, all who see it begin to mock him, saying, 'This man began to build and was not able to finish'?"*
> **Luke 14:28-30**

Not far from where I used to live, a local pastor caught a vision to build a new place of worship. Knowing they didn't have the money to actually build, he took a unique approach. He led the congregation to purchase a beautiful piece of property, clear it and make it build ready. He felt that if the people could see this great work beginning, they would become enthused, begin giving, and the project would eventually be completed.

That was more than seven years ago. I was told that they finally concluded the vision was too big, and the people were not going to fund it. They eventually settled for building an outdoor pavilion for church picnics.

How does a story this sad happen? Lack of preparation.

Now, I want you to listen carefully. Maybe you look back and wonder, "Do I have some unfinished projects in my rearview mirror? Did I fail to follow through because I lacked preparation? Has my past somehow disqualified me for a blessed future?" If that's how you're feeling, you need to hear this: Nothing from your past can prevent God from fulfilling the future he has for you! In fact, the very experiences you've gone through, the successes and failures, they are going to be used by God to do his next work in your life. The only question you have to answer is, "Am I willing to go there with him?"

The very experiences you've gone through, successes and failures, are going to be used by God to do his next work in your life.

Let's circle back to the title of this chapter: Movement Requires Stillness. Sometimes, before you can move you must be still. A command to be still may mean to take a season of time to listen, to get the proper counsel, to obtain understanding. Maybe God needs you to develop in certain areas so that when you reach the next season of great accomplishments, you are able to steward it well.

It's harder when God says wait than when He gives you clear direction and a green light to move. When you have direction, you can get excited and begin to plan. When the command is to wait, the enemy likes to provide you with a multitude of feelings like abandonment, frustration, impatience, despair. Don't listen to the enemy or given in to these emotions. The wisdom of Solomon, a great builder, helps us in these circumstances:

> *Trust in the LORD with all thine heart; and lean not unto thine own understanding. In all thy ways acknowledge him, and he shall direct thy paths.* **Proverbs 3:5-6**

9

Movement Requires Anointing

You prepare a table before me in the presence of my enemies;
You anoint my head with oil; My cup runs over.
Surely goodness and mercy shall follow me
All the days of my life;
And I will dwell in the house of the Lord
Forever.
Psalm 23:5-6 (NKJV)

I believe that Scripture teaches us that there is a critical connection between anointing and movement. What do I mean? Put simply, the anointing of the Holy Spirit is absolutely critical if we want to move in a way that God will bless. Some readers might not know what I mean by "the anointing." In the next few pages, I hope you'll come to understand.

The word is rooted in the Old Testament practice of pouring olive oil over the head of a future king, symbolizing God's call on that person's life. The New Testament teaches that *all* believers receive the Holy Spirit. It also teaches that we are given a specific calling and gifting of the Holy Spirit. In other words, just like a King was called into a particular anointing, so are you. When you walk in that anointing, you will experience incredible blessing. At the heart of all this is the promise of God, our Father, who has a sovereign plan for your life, a calling, that he has anointed you to accomplish! Discovering that anointing will lead you into the kind of movement that God honors.

Anointing and Confidence

King David went through a very long and difficult journey getting to the throne. He went through as many emotional trials as he did physical ones. Before God did anything with David, he marched him out in front of the entire military force of Israel and had him take on the country's worst enemy, alone.

Single-handedly David defeated a ruthless giant that was staring down the entire army. In one day, God took David's reputation from being that of a shepherd to that of giant-slayer. In fact, after this transpired, the women from every town in Israel came out dancing and singing: "Saul has slain his thousands, and David his tens of thousands."

I don't believe David would have walked out there had he not known that God's hand of protection was on him. How did he know this? Well, just before David's encounter with Goliath, God had sent the prophet Samuel to anoint him as the next King of Israel.

David was able to take on Goliath because he knew he had been chosen by God and anointed by the prophet to lead this nation. Knowing that God had placed him in this position, he was confident that God would be with him.

Before you step out into movement, you should know two things:

1. That you are anointed
2. What you are anointed to do

People who operate in the area of their anointing wield a confidence that is unmistakable. They have an inner understanding that God is working for them because he is the one that gave them their assignment.

Anointing and Identity

On the day that Jesus preached his first sermon, he walked into a synagogue, stood up, unrolled the scroll of the prophet Isaiah and began to read;

> *"The spirit of the Lord is upon me because, He hath anointed me to preach the gospel to the poor, to heal the broken hearted to set at Liberty them that are bruised...."*
> **Luke 4:18**

Here was another man who knew the same two things as King David. He knew he was anointed by God, and he knew what he was anointed to do. How was this man expressing that he was the Son of God sent to slay the giant of sin? Because Jesus knew *who he was*.

He not only knew because of those words in Isaiah. He knew because on the day he was baptized in the Jordan River, the heavens parted, the Holy Spirit came down and the voice of God said, "This is my beloved Son." Remember, anointing with oil was a symbol of the Holy Spirit. You see, there is a strong link between anointing and identity.

Anointing and Acceleration

Operating within the realm of our anointing gives us confidence. It bestows a sense of identity, but it does even more. It can actually *accelerate* the move of God in our lives.

For example, studying the likes of Smith Wigglesworth, Aimee Semple McPherson or Kathryn Kuhlman, you will find that many miracles of physical healing took place during their ministries. Injuries that might have taken weeks to heal would be instantly whole again. Why? Because the anointing can accelerate a process.

When you make movements inside your calling, you will see things progress with much more speed, fluency and success. I've seen it in my own life. The acceleration of anointing promoted me from a mostly volunteer position at a local church to CEO of a multi-million-dollar destination resort.

Here is what is so interesting to me. Initially, I did not know I was anointed for this kind of work. This realization flowed out of a painful process in my life.

I'll never forget resigning my position as a lead pastor of a church. It was not due to a moral failure or mishap of any kind. I simply was acutely aware that while I was anointed to carry the gospel, teach and preach, I was not anointed to be the pastor of that church. This left me in a state of soul searching. In the midst of that low point, I sought counsel from a trusted pastor of a local mega church. During our discussion he mentioned that God might be calling me to the business world. I immediately, and defensively, stated that I felt called only to do ministry. At that time I thought it was an either/or option. He was the first to suspect that God had ministry *and* business in mind for my future.

Over the next few years God allowed me to experience multiple disappointments and dissatisfaction with full-time ministry. Not ministry itself, but rather the pursuit of doing it full time. You see, the Lord had a process he needed me to go through, a journey to discover my true anointing. Initially, I thought it was taking me outside of God's anointing on my life. Realistically, it was preparing me for a greater level of ministry.

God had to reveal where I *wasn't* anointed before I could find out where I *was*. He led me into a season where it seemed no doors were opening for me. I had no idea what direction to take. I feared making the wrong move. I felt paralyzed.

Then, on one particular Sunday morning after a service, a woman approached me as I walked off the platform and said she wanted me to meet a businessman who owned multiple businesses in town. She said she believed I was going to be the CEO of his company. She didn't just *suggest* it, she *prophesied* it.

You might as well have told me I would be the first astronaut to walk on Mars.

Twelve months later, I was sitting behind an executive desk as the CEO of a multimillion-dollar destination resort. I had struggled while striving to fulfill my call to full-time ministry. Then God revealed I was anointed for a hybrid of callings.

When you make

MOVEMENTS

inside your calling,
you will see things

PROGRESS

with much more

SPEED,
FLUENCY
and SUCCESS.

It wasn't because of my education. It wasn't because I had a great network. It wasn't because I was in a family that could pass this down to me. It was because God had revealed my anointing. There are times when God will pick the most unqualified person and then qualify that person so that man can't get the glory, only He can.

When that lady prophesied over me that I would be elevated in the business world, I didn't have the faith to believe in that word for myself. She believed it for me! Sometimes, God will surround you with people who see an anointing on you that you can't see on yourself.

I didn't know it at the time, but that step into the business world was just the first one on an incredible journey. You see, God was preparing to raise me to a position of coaching some of the greatest ministers in the country on a full-time basis. The moment I discovered my anointing, I was moved there more quickly than I could have imagined!

Anointing, Where Faith and Works Meet

For many believers, there is a struggle to balance faith and works. What does it mean to trust God? What does it mean to be responsible? How can I throw myself into my work without falling into the trap of trying to do things in my own strength? Is there a way I can pursue accomplishment without surrendering God's favor?

I think this is precisely the place where anointing comes in. Understanding our anointing allows us to work with all our heart while pleasing the heart of God. Why? Because living in the anointing means having the eyes to see the supreme importance of resting in God's favor and doing the work it takes to see it flourish!

I grew up in a ministry environment in which everything was spiritualized. There was no balance of faith with works. Everything was focused on faith. We believed God for everything; from the food we would eat to the retirement we would enjoy. We believed that God held it all in his hands. God was in control. End of story. This tended to create an atmosphere of passive faith.

Then I became exposed to an environment where God was not mentioned in the scenario. Everything was about our individual works. Work hard. Make a living. Make good career choices. Make good business decisions, and you will enjoy the fruits of your labor. God was nowhere to be found when it came to that fruit! Everything relied upon our will to work, our education, our experience and our network.

The fact is, there is a balance between the two that many of us strive to find daily in our life.

For spiritually minded people, there is sometimes a measure of guilt that will come along with their desire to pursue financial prosperity, or a prosperous career, or a prosperous education. They somehow equate prosperity with spiritual compromise. They can fall into the trap of simply "waiting on the Lord" to bring blessing that he, in fact, gave them the ability to produce themselves!

For some who are business-minded, entrepreneurs, CEOs or stockbrokers, everything can be very logical. They look at the spreadsheet and say, "If I do this, I will get that." They might not factor in the blessing of God at all. They look at numbers and say, "Data doesn't lie." For these folks, the danger is falling into a trap sometimes called "functional atheism." Of course, I don't mean that they don't believe in God. I just mean they function as if his existence is not a factor in their financial life. There is a balance.

There is a place where faith coupled with works can bring great results and great destiny. When you bring your faith and your works together you open the door for God to put his super on your natural. Now you have the best of your world and the best of God's world together. When God puts a blessing on your natural, your best becomes supernatural.

This is what it means to operate in the power of anointing. When we pour ourselves out, passionately moving forward in the sphere that God has given us, amazing things happen. That sphere of anointing is like a "can't fail if you try" playground! Not because you'll never fall or make a mistake, but because every single fall in pursuit of God's purposes is, in the end, still a move in the right direction. That "failure" will end up being a part of your future blessing!

The best picture I can paint for you of all this is that of a toddler, just learning to walk. Have you ever seen one of those videos on YouTube? It's amazing, isn't it? Those little fellas hold their arms up over their heads. Every second step, it looks like they might crash. Soon, they finally trip and fall down.

When that happens, dad doesn't yell. He doesn't get disappointed. He cheers them on and helps them up. Why?

Because they're doing what they were made to do. They're just learning how to do it well.

This is what it means to move forward in the anointing. Do what God has anointed you to do, and even when you land on your backside, your Father will cheer because you're moving in the right direction!

It is in this state that God will give you favor. This will impact everything in your life—work, relationships, finances and so much more. You are called to move. Be sure you're moving in the anointing.

10

Movement Requires Risk

Now in the fourth watch of the night Jesus went to them, walking on the sea. And when the disciples saw Him walking on the sea, they were troubled, saying, "It is a ghost!" And they cried out for fear. But immediately Jesus spoke to them, saying, "Be of good cheer! It is I; do not be afraid." And Peter answered Him and said, "Lord, if it is You, command me to come to You on the water." So He said, "Come." **Matthew 14:25-29 (NKJV)**

We live in a risk-averse society. It wasn't always that way. When I grew up, we rode our bikes without helmets. We played with firecrackers and shot BB guns. We climbed trees as close to the top as we could possibly get. Moms would send their kids out on a summer's day and have no clue where they were until it was time for dinner. Now, it seems like kids are bundled in bubble wrap, scheduled to the second and tracked on their smart phones any moment they're not within view of mom and dad.

In this environment, it is easy to equate risk with irresponsibility. That can be true of certain risks, but we can't miss this truth: Some risks are required if we want to keep up with the Holy Spirit. In fact, God loves it when we're willing to take a risk for the right reasons.

Our willingness to risk doesn't obligate God to do anything, but it does please him! Just as the farmer must sow seed into the ground, surrendering it, so we must also surrender our treasures to obtain God's blessing. We must be willing to risk our dreams, our time, our energy and our comfort zone if we have any hope of moving in a way that God will honor.

Hobart Assembly – A risk worth taking!

A while ago, I had the privilege of serving as a consultant for a church in Hobart Indiana. At the time, Pastor Ryan had been leading and growing the congregation at Hobart Assembly for more than ten years. Because of their growth, they needed to expand their facilities. Parking was limited, children's space was maxed out, administrative space was tiny and a new worship facility essential.

After an extensive financial analysis, it turned out their need was bigger than their financial capacity. I want to take this opportunity to say something here. Nearly every pastor I have worked with had a vision that was greater than the apparent provision. Any real pastor experiences this problem, but financial provision always follows a God-birthed vision.

Pastor Ryan is a faith teacher. I explained to him that the vision was larger than their resources. He looked at me and started speaking faith. He quoted scripture and said, "I don't know how, but God is going to do this."

We took the vision to the leaders. They agreed, we needed to take a risk! In faith, they took the vision to the congregation, and God's people responded. They got so fired up they surpassed what 95% of churches with their giving trend could do.

Then an email showed up in their inbox. Their neighboring property owner had a well-established ministry and was offering it to them at a fair price with positive cash flow. She even offered to finance it for them, and the deal included the lease tenant who had a 28-year lease history there. This arrangement would provide them with revenue to help fund the vision God had given them! They took the deal, and the newly acquired positive cash flow began to help fund the project.

God was only getting started. He began sending people from all over the nation to help. In one particular instance, a man and his family were transferred by his employer to their area all the way from Florida. This didn't make sense to the man because he worked remotely from his home. As soon as he walked into Hobart Assembly, however, he immediately recognized why the transfer had taken place. He was on assignment from God to help the ministry. His family is now a major part of the miracle.

Reflecting on God's provision, Pastor Ryan said, "Never forget that God is a strategic God. He knows how to fund His Kingdom and how to position His resources."

This is what I call God-honoring risk.

Why do people not move?

Christians sometimes have their own language for things. I've heard it called "Christianese." Sometimes, it's just an "insider" way of saying something that outsiders wouldn't understand. Many times it is not more than a Christians escape from taking action. Here are some of those statements: "God will work it all out," "Just pray about it," or "Wait on the Lord." You get the idea.

While there is some truth to all of these statements, many have been severely overplayed and become, by default, an escape strategy. If you want to take no action, any one of these statements will do just fine. While these things sound real spiritual, they are many times a psychological green light to remain dormant. Unfortunately, some people value sounding spiritual more than getting something done.

I've heard people say, "Just wait and the right door will open up." Again, while in some situations this is indeed the right approach to take, I believe that many times this is what we say when we don't know how to figure out what to do next. So, why do we fear movement?

Some people refuse to risk because they have a fear of not succeeding. There's a plethora of books and one-liners that deal with this, so I won't bore you with telling you things you already know. I will say this: It would be a shame if you lived your whole life dreaming great things and never acting on them because you thought you might not be successful.

Others refuse to risk because they aren't familiar with the territory they are dreaming about. It's difficult to map out a plan of approach when you don't know the geography you're navigating. Sometimes it's necessary to place people around you that have been down the road you want to go down. They can help you plan a strategy that will lead to success while navigating around common missteps.

This is why I hired consultants when I was the CEO of a destination resort. I had never gone down that path and didn't have the luxury to make mistakes. I needed to get it right the first time. For more than a year I surrounded myself with consultants. I had a consultant with me six days a week, sixteen hours a day. It was a no-holds-barred crash course, and we trained at Mach 1 speed with our hair on fire.

Common Denominators

While we could keep adding reasons to this list, there are two major common denominators that I see keeping people from risk: Fear and complacency. You can list a hundred reasons that people don't move and usually boil them down to these two root causes.

Fear has all kinds of family members like anxiety, low self-esteem, lack of self-confidence, anticipation of failure, and anticipation of rejection.

Complacency on the other hand has its family as well: Procrastination, laziness, lack of interest, poor attention span, lack of discipline, lack of commitment, distraction, and lack of intellectual curiosity

In Scripture, Jesus prayed for the sick. Sometimes he prayed that they would be healed, other times he rebuked a spirit of infirmity. One was a natural root to the problem while another was a spiritual root. Jesus had the brilliant discernment of knowing which was the cause of someone's illness. This discernment gave Him the wisdom to know how to pray to get the desired result. Could it be that, at times, we don't see our prayers answered because we do not first seek to understand the root of the issue?

Like sickness, I believe that fear and complacency can be spirits. I also believe they can also be natural traits passed down generationally or developed over time. Sometimes these spirits or natural traits are effective at keeping us from getting started while other times they cause us to give up halfway, before we can succeed. Sometimes these spirits are successful at just bogging us down and slowing our pace to such a degree that we never accomplish anything of importance.

The Danger of Distraction

Distraction is one of the most successful weapons the enemy uses against Christians. Satan likes to get us so wrapped up in our personal problems and issues that we never get involved at the level that we should in Kingdom business.

Don't get bogged down by trying to work out the full picture before you get started. In many cases you will never see the end picture until the actual end. In the meantime, simply start where you are and give it all you have. If Steve Jobs would have tried to figure out all the products he was going to make, how they were going to work and how he was going to market them before he started Apple, he would have never set up shop in a garage. What he did was start where he was and let the rest unfold. So first, we got the Apple Macintosh, and then eventually we got the iPhone. I'm not encouraging lack of vision. You must have a clear, crisp, and compelling vision to get started, but don't get so caught up in details that it paralyzes you from getting started. Sometimes, our need for all the answers is just a distraction from taking that risk.

Don't get bogged down by trying to work out the full picture before you get started.

Some try to fly before they walk. They map out this massive dream that would take unprecedented miracles and deep pocket investors to bring it to reality. Scaling back vision into stages and phases that are realistic and attainable can help keep you from being overwhelmed. It will also keep you from exhausting yourself trying to launch something that is beyond your capacity to get off the ground.

How do we know we should risk?

Some risks are logical and simple. For example, if you need more financial security a good way to start is to spend less than you make. If you desire to be in better health, you begin by eating better and exercising. Here, the only risk is being willing to change.

On the other hand, some risks are tremendously complicated and challenging. There are times that you will have great vision and dreams that bring with them corresponding questions regarding next steps. These can be times of great supernatural challenge. Sometimes, the risk will place such a demand on God's anointing that you must first spend much time in prayer, consultation and studying God's heart. It is in these times that we must ask for clear instruction. In times like these, risk without revelation can result in exhausting motion without great rewards.

The Israelites had one of these complicated and challenging needs. There was an entire city standing between them and their promised land. They sought instruction from God. God, in turn, instructed the Israelites that their next move was to march around Jericho. By all accounts this type of movement seems trivial and simplistic in comparison to the army and fortress they were up against. The important note here is the instructions came from God. The risk of looking silly was worth it!

When you determine that you are going to seek God's voice for your next steps, you must be submitted in your heart that you will do whatever He assigns you. Sometimes His leading will come to you in a clear inner voice that you recognize as God's direction. Other times it will come through wise counsel. Whether it is simple or complicated, it will bring the desired results.

Three Guiding Lights

There are three guiding lights I have noticed that pastors, leaders, and believers look for when making big decisions.

1. **Peace.** The decisions must be accompanied by an inner peace about moving forward. The anticipated journey might have you a little

nervous, but you have peace in knowing that is the right direction.

2. **Confirmation.** Let every word be established out of the mouth of two or three witnesses. When God is speaking, you will find that he will confirm it to you. You might open a piece of mail, and it is stating exactly what God has been saying to you. You might hear a sermon that clearly confirms what you are feeling. Maybe it's a song, but God will find a way to confirm his word to you.
3. **Counsel.** There is safety in a multitude of counselors. Listening to others who have been down the same road you are on can help you navigate a variety of land mines. You can also find a level of security in hearing that the crazy times you might be experiencing along the way are not only to be expected, but normal.

God Rewards Risky Faith

Previous to the Israelites destroying Jericho with a simple march, they had to get across the Jordan River. God gave them a simple command: Let the priests go forth. He made an audacious promise: *And as soon as the priests who carry the ark of the Lord – the Lord of all the earth – set foot in the Jordan, its waters flowing downstream will be cut off and stand up in a heap.* **Joshua 3:13** (NIV)

All they had to do was be willing to risk. Not only did God honor their movement, but he also told them what move to make to receive the specific result. Sometimes God will tell you what to do and what will happen when you do it. This is the best scenario. He provides direction and anticipates you to follow through with it committing to perform on your behalf if you do what he has asked.

Spiritual Diversions

When you begin to step out in risk, God is not the only one that will begin to honor your movement. Satan might take note of your movement as well. He will sometimes tempt you with a false sense of urgency to fool you with the fake before the real is produced. He knows Scripture and God's ways as well as we do. He knows that once you begin to put action behind your faith, God is going to provide things for you. His last-ditch effort is to deceive you into settling. When evaluating your options, you must pray for discernment to understand if it is God that is honoring your movement or Satan that is motivating your movement.

I want this moment to be an alert to someone that is tempted to settle for less than God's best. Do not settle! You cannot pray without God hearing you. You cannot seek his will without him taking notice and providing you guidance. God has heard your prayers and he is working *for* you not against you. As you honor God, he will honor you. Don't settle for less than what you have been believing and praying for. Then take that risk!

11

Movement Requires Resilience

People do not despise a thief if he steals to satisfy himself when he is starving.
Yet when he is found, he must restore sevenfold; He may have to give up all the substance of his house.
Proverbs 6:30-31

And from the days of John the Baptist until now the kingdom of heaven suffers violence, and the violent take it by force.
Matthew 11:12

All of us have gone through seasons where things that belonged to us were ripped away. Through the school of hard knocks, we have learned that life sometimes isn't fair. It might be a career opportunity, a real estate deal, a missed investment opportunity or even a lost loved one. Whatever the loss, we have all felt the pain.

Sometimes there is nothing you can do when things are taken from you. When I was eight years old, my father was taken from me. He died of a brain aneurysm. I couldn't bring him back. As a young child I felt incredibly helpless, unable to change what had just happened.

Then something happened that might have changed everything.

In the midst of our grief, as our family gathered at my father's wake, I remember seeing a well-known missionary appear. This man had just been to our church. His stories had gripped our hearts. One, in particular, came to mind in that moment. You see, that missionary had given a testimony of how he had raised someone from the dead in a foreign country.

My spirits soared when he showed up to pay his respects to my father. I pictured him walking up to that casket, taking my dad by the hand and commanding the life back into his body.

It didn't happen.

Unfortunately, there are things we all face that are completely out of our control. They are beyond our ability to understand and we must release them into the hands of God and trust him that he sees the big picture and works all things together for our good.

Bill and the Thief

Much later in life I bought a house and was doing renovations. The formal room had a 16-foot-high ceiling where I wished to install crown molding. I rented scaffolding from the local home improvement store and invited my brother and two other friends to give me a hand.

It was a warm Saturday afternoon when we set up our tools on the driveway. The garage door was raised, and I had a Miter saw and other random tools set up.

Atop the scaffold, I measured and called out the appropriate size board needed, and my friend Bill would run out and cut it. He would then carry it in the house, and my other friend Eric would hand it up to me.

Bill had just brought a board into the house and handed it off to Eric. He turned and headed back out to the saw with my new requested measurements in mind. Less than ninety seconds later, I heard Bill yelling my name at the top of his lungs: "Jeff! Jeff! Jeff!"

I was immediately alarmed, as were Eric and my brother Jack. I half-slid, half-scampered down the scaffold, tools spilling out of my jostled toolbelt and down onto the hardwood floor.

Running outside, the first thing I felt was confused. Bill was walking down the sidewalk towards my house. In his arms, he carried a milk crate with miscellaneous items spilling out. Over his shoulder was my Stihl backpack leaf blower. He was red in the face and yelling, "That guy just robbed you!"

My mind was now racing. I was trying to put the scene together. I didn't see any "guy." There was no person or car within eyesight. Where did this stuff come from in his arms? Why was he carrying my blower? How did he get that far up the street when he literally just walked out my front door?

I ran to help off-load some of his burden. He handed me the milk crate. "What in the world is going on?" I asked. He waved his arm up the street and quickly explained that when he exited the house, he saw an SUV parked by the curb about 100 ft away. There was a guy running out of my garage with my blower. He ran to the vehicle, tossed it into the back of the SUV and was jumping in the driver's seat.

There's something you need to know about Bill to understand what happened next. Bill has a military background. He's physically fit, sharp and has a lot of street smarts. In other words, he's wired and trained for action.

Bill immediately recognized what was happening and leaped off the porch in a dead run towards the criminal's SUV. He jumped onto the back of the vehicle while the thief sat stunned staring into his rearview mirror. He was trying to put the getaway car into gear but was apparently briefly paralyzed by Bill's aggression.

Bill, having missed a few church services, was screaming expletives at him while grabbing my blower. It was then that he decided getting my blower was not good enough; that good-for-nothing thief needed to pay for his crimes. That was the split second he decided to grab anything else he could get his hands on. First the milk crate, then some bolt cutters and even a license plate lying next to it. In a split second, he shoved it all into the crate and jumped off.

The thief opened his driver's door as though he were about to engage Bill, then, thinking better of it, he slammed his door closed. He threw his van into gear and peeled off, racing towards safety from this unpredictable mad man.

Bill was fired up! Jack, Eric and I were all on the sidewalk surrounding Bill. He was now on his knees digging through the milk crate, triumphant over his spoils. He had a set of drill bits, hand tools, bungee cords, shop rags, the bolt cutters, and of course, my leaf blower. He was still talking in rushed elevated tones.

He said, "I've always told myself that if I was ever robbed, I would not only get my stuff back, but I would also take the thief's stuff as well, and I just did it!" He was exuberant.

Bill refused to be a victim. He had the spirit of "fight back." He is not the type to sit by and let things be ripped out of his possession. When things went south, he quickly leapt into aggressive action, and took things back, plus some.

Proverbs 6:31 says when the thief is found he must restore seven times what he stole. If Bill had not moved fast and taken the leap onto that SUV, I would have lost possession of what was rightfully mine.

There are times that you lose things, and it is of no fault of yours. There are also times you can actually do something about things that have been taken from you. Too many times we sit around and nurse the pain of loss rather than stirring up the fight for restoration.

Understanding when to move, and move with aggression, is many times the key to what could be a short window of opportunity. Don't hesitate to defend what is rightfully yours.

Favor from a Bank

A friend of mine is a Bishop at a large urban church. This is a church that seats thousands, a great monument to what God can do when people unite and work to see the Kingdom advanced.

Construction was completed just previous to the economic downturn of 2008-2009. The congregation had participated in multiple capital campaigns and saved money for years. Those resources, combined with a generous loan from the bank, made it possible for them to move into this palatial edifice. The church is centrally located in one of the neediest areas of the city, right next to a major interstate.

Just as they were moving in, the economy collapsed. The housing market crashed, the stock market plummeted and businesses, great and small, shuttered their doors.

Unfortunately, this impacted a large portion of their congregation. Great local corporations that employed the parishioners downsized or ceased to exist. Almost overnight, the income of this mammoth ministry drastically dropped. Few could have foreseen such a collapse.

The Bishop decided to refinance the building. A better rate could reduce their overhead by thousands of dollars each week. The bank had other plans. They had taken a beating from the recession as well. They appraised the building at millions less than what it was financed for and refused to refinance without large sums of cash down.

The Bishop spoke with a loan consultant. He was a Spirit-filled man and promised to do everything he could to help them out. He connected with the bank and proposed every scenario possible. Six months went by, then ten, then twelve. There was no progress made.

Eighteen months later I sat down with the Bishop in his office. It was clear that he had given up what had only been a faint hope from the beginning. He knew, after talking with the bank for several years himself and getting nowhere, that it was unlikely things would ever change, even with a great loan consultant.

His only option was to begin making small steps forward. He decided to embark on a Capital Campaign. He knew the money raised during this campaign would be a far cry from what the church needed, but he had to do something. He couldn't just sit there and wait, hoping for things to change.

I met with his leadership team and found them to be incredible high-capacity leaders. Due to financial constraints, they were understaffed. Each one was serving in several different roles. I marveled at how excited each staff member was to know that God was using them to do incredible work in unprecedented times.

Together, we mapped out a timeline of events to execute a campaign. We could feel God's undeniable presence in the room as we discussed the seemingly impossible financial burden.

Less than two months later, the Bishop's phone rang. It was the mortgage consultant. He had reached a deal with the bank. They had agreed to reduce the amount of money owed to them.

This was a huge breakthrough, but it wasn't the full provision that they were hoping to see. The amount the bank was willing to reduce the note was still not enough to get them below the appraisal value. Still, it was something, and at this point, the Bishop felt any progress would be a win. He determined to sign the paperwork immediately.

The loan consultant pushed back. He felt that God was going to do something greater and asked the Bishop to give him some additional time.

In the end, a miracle happened. The bank agreed to forgive millions of dollars of debt which, in turn, brought the remaining balance owed below the appraised value.

This was an absolute miracle! Unprecedented. This was God intervening at a level at which even the bank president himself said had never been done in the history of their business.

It took ten years. A solid decade passed following the loss of this church's appraisal value, its income, and many of its parishioners.

Yet when the Bishop decided to make the biggest move he could make, begin a campaign, God started moving. The impossible became possible. The closed doors were flung open. The "no" was replaced with "yes." God honored movement.

The Four Lepers

In II Kings 7, we read of four leprous men that dwelt just outside the gates of Samaria. In those days if you were diagnosed with leprosy, you became an outcast and were sent out of the city to dwell in colonies with others of the same fatal malady.

Leprosy is contagious, an infectious disease that eats away at your skin. It affects the respiratory tract, the peripheral nerves and even the eyes, sometimes leading to paralysis of the hands and feet. If you have ever seen a picture of someone battling this, you will never forget it.

Ben-Hadad, King of Aram, had marched in his troops and surrounded the city of Samaria. No one could leave or enter. This created a terrible famine for the Samaritans. They were dying of starvation.

The lepers also had no food and were without hope. They decided that, rather than wait for death to come to them, they would get up and walk over to the camp of Aram and see if they would give them food. The chances of being killed by the enemy were pretty high but they knew they were going to die slowly of starvation anyway. Why not take a chance on the soldiers having pity on them?

Just after the sun went down, the lepers decided to make their move. In 2 Kings 7:6, the Bible tells us that as the lepers were shuffling towards the enemy camp, God caused their movements to have the sound of mighty armies with marching men and horses.

The warriors of the army of Aram panicked and ran for their lives, abandoning everything. When the lepers arrived, there was no one to be found. All the food, clothing, gold, and personal possessions were waiting for them to possess.

It was an incredible day for the lepers. They were immediately well fed and quite wealthy. How did this happen? They got up and moved. That is it. God did the rest. They refused to give up. They were resilient.

While there are legitimate times that we lose things and can do nothing about it, there are also times we have an opportunity to fight back. Recognizing and seizing those opportunities is critical to holding on to the blessings God has for you. While my friend Bill had the energy to run and fight back, the lepers barely had the strength to walk. Whatever your situation, just do what you can and watch God move for you.

Isaiah 40:31 shares these words of hope: "*But they that wait on the LORD shall renew their strength; they shall mount up with wings as eagles; they shall run, and not be weary; and they shall walk, and not faint.*"

The enemy of your breakthrough always reigns in fear with the purpose of paralyzing you.

The enemy of your breakthrough always reigns in fear with the purpose of paralyzing you. It wants to keep you from moving. Once you truly understand that even the slightest move catches God's attention and evokes His response on your behalf, nothing will be able to stop you.

12

Get Moving

Your ears shall hear a word behind you, saying,
"This is the way, walk in it,"
Whenever you turn to the right hand
Or whenever you turn to the left.
Isaiah 30:21 (NKJV)

Think about this for a second: Billy Graham had a Sunday School teacher who led him to Jesus Christ. That nameless saint took the time to make a move. They took a step of faith and impacted a young boy who one day would lead hundreds of thousands of people to faith in Jesus. That is the power of movement.

As I think about the power of movement, I want to close out this book by challenging you to make the most important movement I can imagine: Move toward other people in such a way that they start moving for Jesus. Take time to see the people around you. Recognize their potential. Realize that God might want you to be the person who gets them moving in the right direction. If you adopt this perspective, you will impact the world in ways you can't begin to imagine.

My own life has been radically impacted by people willing to move. I've shared some of those stories here. Other people have moved in my life, leading me to make moves. Personally, I'm stunned that God has used me the way he has. There's nothing special about my life. Only one thing has made all the difference: When God moved in me, I was willing to help other people get moving.

Get Out of the Car

I was 19 and driving from my childhood home in Maryland to Mississippi where I was attending Bible College. I was a few hours into my trip, traveling along the long stretch of winding road through the mountains of Virginia. If you've ever been on this stretch of Interstate 81, you know it is beautiful with mountains, fields and forest as far as the eye can see. You also know that one can drive for a very great distance before you see any signs of civilization.

I was in my 1985 dark blue Ford Escort. It was my first car. My boss, Mack, who owned the local convenience store where I worked, had been kind enough to give me my first car loan to purchase it. I liked his kind of loan because he handed me a huge wad of cash and told me to offer the dealer $2,300 for the car. I had never held that much money before. It was a wonderful feeling. The dealer was asking $2,600, and I wasn't sure he would settle for less. The cash, however, placed a lot of confidence in my step so I shoved it in the cargo pocket of my Bugle Boy jeans and drove to the car lot. The car salesman gladly accepted, and I drove away in my beautiful dark blue 4-speed Ford Escort.

Mack took a personal interest in investing in me as a person. This was rare and a blessing to a teenage boy who didn't have a father. On several occasions, we would open up the store at 6:00 a.m. and get business going. When the next shift came in, he would take me to Denny's for a late breakfast. There he would proceed to talk with me about all kinds of interesting things. The kind of things that a dad would discuss with his son. He would lecture me about furthering my education and encourage me to start a family one day. He would explain that I was a good employee for him because I was trustworthy and connected well with his customers. He said they liked me and that was good for business.

I remember one morning sitting at the table, I had just ordered my usual Grand Slam when he began to talk with me about love and relationships. He explained that when he met his wife and asked her father if he could marry her, he loved her with all he had in him. It had been more than twenty years since their wedding, and he said he loved her more now than he did when he married her. I asked him how that was possible since he loved her as much as possible from the start of their marriage.

He explained it like this. Love is never stagnant. It either grows or wilts. For love to grow, your capacity for love must expand. Doing life together and loving through the good times and the difficult times increases your capacity. The last twenty plus years had done just that. The life they had lived out together had expanded his capacity to love her well beyond the day he looked her in the eyes at the altar.

I will never forget the day he found out I was going 1,000 miles away to college. He was so happy and proud of me. He and his wife took me out to dinner and handed me another wad of cash. He wanted me to have money for the things I would need at college. He also graciously forgave me of the remaining balance on my car loan.

That man was a Godsend in more ways than one. He always gave me work when I returned home for holidays and summer breaks. Without his support along with multiple jobs on and off campus, I would have never been able to fund my tuition.

So now let me get back to my road trip.

I was coasting along quite nicely, enjoying the scenery of Virginia when I heard a strange noise coming from the front passenger side. I pulled off to the side of the road, climbed out of the car and walked around to see if I could spot something out of the ordinary. There it was: Two of the four lugs on the wheel had broken off! The lugs and nuts both were somewhere alongside the road back down the interstate. With only two lugs remaining, and no exit anywhere in sight I elected to drive the car as slowly as possible on the shoulder of the road until I could find an exit with a filling station or at least a pay phone.

I placed the car in drive and drove only a few feet when I heard a third lug snap off with a loud pop. Apparently, continuing was not a good idea unless I wanted my right front wheel to fly out from under my car, dropping my chassis on the pavement.

There was no civilization in my line of sight for as far as I could see. I realized I was going to need to make a move I had never made before. My mother would have certainly been worried had she known what I was doing, but I had made up my mind. I would hitchhike.

I grabbed my Day Planner, locked the car and started walking. I had not walked 1,000 feet from my car when the first vehicle emerged from around the bend. It was a large 18-wheeler roaring down on me. I turned to walk backwards and stuck out my thumb. Almost immediately I could hear the truck begin to slow, the engine roaring deeply as the driver downshifted. He pulled over several yards ahead. I could hear the hiss of the air brakes as I jogged up to the cab. I jumped up on the sideboard and opened the door. There was a middle-aged greying man with pleasant features behind the wheel. He called out in a slight southern accent, "Climb on in!"

I jumped inside, and he held out his hand. "I'm Fred Lautenbach," he said.

"Jeff Shortridge," I replied. As he began working the big lumbering rig through its lower gears, conversation immediately ensued.

"Where are you coming from?" he asked.

"Maryland," I replied.

"Where you going?"

"Mississippi," I answered.

"That's where I live!" he responded. "What part are you going to?"

"Jackson. I'm a student at a Bible college there and am heading back from summer break."

"Well I live about three hours from there in a town called Tupelo." Fred responded.

I was surprised to say the least. "My mother lives in Tupelo," I said. "She moved there a year ago and works at a children's orphanage."

It was his turn to express surprise. "Which children's orphanage?" he quickly asked.

"Tupelo's Children's Mansion," I replied.

The look of disbelief in his eyes was priceless. "My wife and I attend the Church that owns that orphanage!"

We both sat stunned for a moment. I-81 is 855 miles long. The portion between the Virginia borders alone is 324 miles. Out of the tens of thousands of cars that zip along Interstate 81 in a single day, what are the chances that he would be passing the same mile marker I was parked at, at the exact time that I decided to get out of the car and put out my thumb? We both immediately knew this was a God moment. God had orchestrated our every move for the last few minutes, hours maybe even days, and brought us together at the perfect time. This man was my guardian angel.

He pulled off at the next exit and guided the truck into a rough-looking garage for big rigs. "They don't work on cars here, but I'm going to talk with them and get them to help you" he said. He walked me through the huge bay door, and before you know it, the manager was ordering the parts I needed.

Not only did that crew of mechanics have the parts specially delivered within the hour, but they also sent a truck out to my car and hauled it into one of their bays. There they drilled out the broken off lugs, re-tapped the holes, and with three new lugs and nuts had my car ready for the road in no time.

I'll never forget Fred. His life had precision guidance by God that day, and he didn't even know it. God made sure he got out of bed at the right time that morning, didn't linger too long at the breakfast table, and drove the precise speed needed to pick me up.

It's amazing when you realize that God prompts us to do things simply because we are His hands, and we are His feet. I wonder how many times you have been guided by God in your smallest decisions and didn't even know it.

I've often thought about this amazing event. What would have happened if I had not made the move to get out of my car and start walking? What if I had been too afraid of some psycho pulling over and not stuck out my thumb? Or what if I had just sat there and prayed and asked God to take control and work it all out?

What I didn't know was He was already working it out. He had started working out my answer when Fred had started that particular run he was on. Every mile he had traveled for the last several days had been timed by God. Where he stopped the night before and slept. What time he woke up the next morning. When he stopped for lunch. Everything he did was timed perfectly by God to place him exactly where God wanted him to be at the right time. All I had to do was get up and meet the answer where God had lined it up to be at the right time. Isaiah 65:24 says, "Before they call, I will answer…" This means that God heard my prayers days before I prayed them and was already working on my behalf!

God

PROMPTS

us to do things
simply because
we are

HIS HANDS

and we are

HIS FEET

This happened in 1990 so we didn't have cell phones yet. If I would have sat in my car that day out of fear or false understanding of how God answers prayer, I would have missed God. What if I had not gotten out of my car and instead waited for a police officer to show up? I may have been there a very long time. What if I had started walking but was too afraid to stick my thumb out?

How hard would it have been for God to get that trucker to pull over and walk back to a parked car on the side of the interstate to see who was inside and if he could help? That probably would never have happened simply because that prompting would have been so far out of the realm of normality for that man, he may have dismissed the thought before it had a chance to materialize.

Sometimes you have to get yourself out there in front of people and in the middle of situations for God to be able to do his thing. Remember, he is dealing with normal people that don't like to get outside of their comfort zone. Most times, he won't just speak and get someone to hunt you up in your neighborhood and walk into your house to bless you as you sit on your couch. That's why *your* movement is so important.

I wonder how many answers to your prayers God has already worked out. Maybe all you have to do is just move, and he will put you in the right place at the right time for your miracle!

This is the power of movement. God honors movement so get moving!

JEFF SHORTRIDGE

One of those rare individuals who has both extensive pastoral experience and solid business acumen, Jeff served in Pastoral ministry for 14 years (including the role of senior pastor) and as the CEO of an exclusive corporate resort and retreat center.

Jeff has been training and leading leaders since 2000 in roles as varied as CEO, Marketing Manager, Real Estate Developer, and Executive Vice President. His business experience ranges from the auto industry to real estate sales to the service industry.

He has a B.A. in Religious Studies and Music and is a gifted communicator who has spoken to numerous business groups and churches alike from coast to coast.

Jeff has been a ministry consultant with INJOY Stewardship Solutions since 2009 and has personally coached more than one hundred churches through campaigns to help them move.

He is married to the bride of his dreams, Milinda and has three children, Austin, Sevana and Tony.

www.GodHonorsMovement.com